ATTAC

FROM THE COCKPIT, No 9

GRAEME ROWAN-THOMSON

Contents

INTRODUCTION *Commander Graeme Rowan-Thomson* 4

REQUIREMENT *Commander Graeme Rowan-Thomson* 6

FROM THE COCKPIT *Commander Graeme Rowan-Thomson* 10

TRIALS AND TESTING 20

   Aeroplane & Armament Experimental Establishment, Royal Aircraft Establishment, 21

      A Grave Danger of Floating *Captain Eric Brown* CBE DSC AFC 22

   787 Naval Air Squadron, Royal Naval Handling Squadron 32

      No Hanging About *Lieutenant-Commander Don Moore-Searson* 32

      Checking on the Machery *Commander R. M. ('Mike') Crosley* DSC* 38

   703 and 700 Naval Air Squadrons 40

FRONT-LINE SQUADRONS *Rear-Admiral Ray Rawbone* CB DSC 44

   800 Naval Air Squadron 46

      The Size of the Biceps *Rear-Admiral Ray Rawbone* CB DSC 46

      Crystals and Snake Climbs *Lieutenant-Commander Don Moore-Searson* 48

      Stripped Clean *Rear-Admiral Ray Rawbone* CB DSC 54

      New Territory *Captain Keith Leppard* CBE 58

      They Can Also Bite *Commander Graeme Rowan-Thomson* 60

   803 Naval Air Squadron 64

      Coming-To at Ten Thousand Feet *Commander Tommy Handley* 64

      Does It Tumble When Ditched? *Captain A. W. ('Hap') Chandler* USN 70

890 Naval Air Squadron 88
   You Can't Take It with Water *Commander Graeme Rowan-Thomson* 88
   Stand to Attention! *Lieutenant-Commander Tommy Young* 94
   Rolling and Gliding *Lieutenant-Commander Tommy Young* 96

TRAINING SQUADRONS 98
702, 718, 736 and 767 Naval Air Squadrons 98
   Mouths Open *Commander J. H. ('Boot') Nethersole* 100
   A Dicey Roll *Commander Giles Binney* OBE 102
   Slightly Hazardous *Captain Jack Worth* 106
   From Lossie to Hal Far *Lieutenant-Commander Brian Giffin* 106

RNVR SQUADRONS 108
1831, 1832 and 1833 Naval Air Squadrons 108
   Pride Before the Fall *Lieutenant Robert Neill* RNVR 110

MISCELLANEOUS UNITS 114

ATTACKERS FOR EXPORT 115

INTRODUCTION

Commander Graeme Rowan-Thomson

THE Supermarine Attacker was the first jet-propelled aircraft to be introduced into the Royal Navy. On the world scene it was by no means the first, the best or the fastest, but within the RN its impact was considerable, not only as an aeroplane but also on the 'side effects' that came with it. The piston-engined era was conducted in general at a much slower pace and at lower altitudes: sortie times were longer, endurance times were greater, ground controllers had time to consider, runways of 1,000 yards were quite sufficient, and everyone used aviation (high-octane) spirit.

Then along came the jet. It is easy to be blasé nowadays when everybody travels by jet aircraft and to ask what all the fuss was about. The basics of flying had not changed, the controls operated in the same way, there was a throttle that the pilot pushed forward if he wanted to go faster and pulled back when he wanted to slow down, but it *was* different—and the differences made flying a jet the most exciting step forward I ever experienced in my flying career. For a start, there was no vibration from a reciprocating engine, just the muffled roar of the jet, and there was no enormous powerplant in front of cockpit, blocking the view (quite a consideration when trying to land on a carrier's deck). In the 'minus column', the throttle response of early jet engines was slower than that of their piston contemporaries, particularly at low power, although when power was applied at slow speeds the pilot was not faced with a condition known in the propeller world as 'torque stalling', wherein the abrupt application of power encouraged the propeller to rotate the aircraft (instead of *vice-versa*) and which, at low speeds, could cause a stall. This was a frequent explanation of accidents to aircraft that were being deck-landed: they were low and slow, and if, in a turn on to the deck, they were waved off they had to apply sudden power.

There were many lessons to be learned all round, and everyone had to do a rapid re-think on a whole range of attitudes and practices. Ground controllers

Below: First-generation British Naval jet aircraft: (from near to far) Hawker Sea Hawk, Supermarine Attacker, De Havilland Sea Vampire and Gloster Meteor trainer.
Opposite: An 800 Squadron Attacker, in the high-drag landing configuration, approaches HMS *Eagle*'s flight deck. This aircraft, WA498, ended its career in spectacular fashion—as related on pages 56-57.

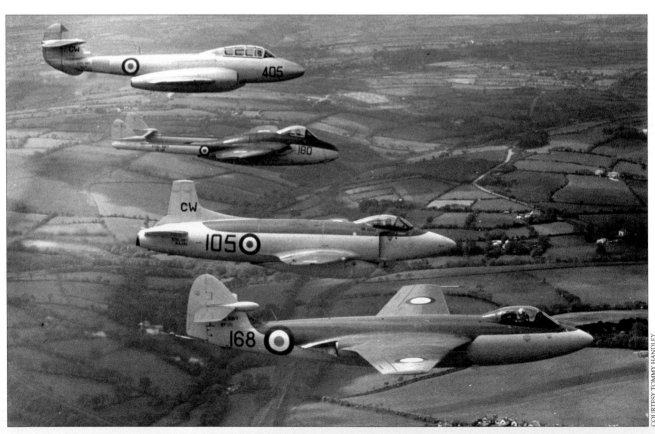

COURTESY PHILIP JARRETT

had to adjust to the fact that the jet moved around the sky a great deal faster than the piston-powered aeroplane and understand that it operated in a wider envelope. When homing aircraft they had to get used to bringing them down from 30,000 feet, with the whole flight pattern taking up more sky and therefore needing greater safety clearances. The other lesson, quickly understood, was that jets did not like hanging around at low level with their wheels and flaps down, in maximum-drag condition. In these circumstances, at low speeds and at low altitudes, fuel consumption went up sharply. Loitering was not popular. There was also a need for a more sophisticated, pilot-interpreted homing system than the current radio beacon, and a faster means of locating and homing aircraft for the ground controllers.

One considerable bonus was that the fuel used by jets was aviation kerosene—a far less volatile and sensitive fuel than petrol with correspondingly less stringent safety measures required when fuelling aircraft. The drawback was the need for aircraft carriers to accommodate large stocks of two types of fuel.

Some of these problems were quickly solved, others, like runway lengths, took time, and it was not until the Attacker's successor, the Sea Hawk, appeared that a pilot-interpreted homing aid was fitted. This was called TACAN—short for Tactical Air Navigator—which comprised a dial calibrated in degrees from 0 to 180 on either side of dead ahead, with an indicator needle and an inset milometer. The pilot could tune the equipment to any military base or carrier and, on picking up a signal from the selected transmitter, the needle would indicate the direction to home in degrees left or right, together with the distance. It could also be used by aircraft to home on each other for the purposes of rendezvous.

The ground controllers were given a radar homing system called FV 10. When a pilot made a transmission, a spike flashed out from the centre of a PPI (plan position indicator), giving the controller a bearing of the aircraft. It could not indicate position, however, so the aircraft had to be homed overhead (indicated by the spike flashing in every direction), whereupon it could be let down on a safe bearing.

REQUIREMENT

Commander Graeme Rowan-Thomson

LONG before it got its name, the Attacker, like most aircraft, started off as a number in a design office—a prototype based on a Staff Requirement. One has to go back to 1944 to find its genesis. Its immediate ancestors in the Supermarine stable were the RAF's Spiteful and the Royal Navy's Seafang, both single-seater piston-engined fighters that were intended as the successors to, respectively, the Spitfire and its 'navalised' cousin the Seafire. They, however, were dropped at the prototype stage when it began to be realised just what the jet engine could do for the performance of fighter aircraft. This was a time when, to an extent, the aircraft engine was leading the airframe design. Rolls-Royce already had the Derwent turbojet powering the Gloster Meteor, and they uprated this with a view to putting it into the prototype aircraft known only as Specification E.1/44. The engine was coded RB.51.

Extensive use was made of experience with the Spiteful/Seafang design and, indeed, three such airframes were modified to take a jet engine. These experimental types satisfied the Ministry of Aircraft Production, who then issued a more precise specification, E.10/44. This was subsequently to become the Attacker, powered by the Rolls-Royce Nene engine of some 5,000 pounds' thrust, and its early development owed a lot to the experience gained in flying the Spiteful prototypes. The designs had many advanced features, and the word 'transonic' was beginning to be used more and more, for the jet had pushed aircraft speeds way beyond the propeller's capability and into the realms where velocity was being measured in relation to the speed of sound—the Mach number. All this was taking place when the international situation was far from stable and a jet-propelled arms race was, very literally, in the air.

Left, upper: The prewar Supermarine Spitfire design—generally accepted as being one of the most outstanding aeronautical concepts ever—was developed and refined throughout the war years and by 1944 had resulted in the 500mph Spiteful (shown). However, it also represented the end of the line for piston-engined fighter aircraft: jets were the future.

Left, lower: The Royal Navy's equivalent of the Spiteful was the Seafang but, like the Spiteful, it did not enter production (although its immediate predecessor the Seafire continued to equip front-line squadrons until 1951 and indeed fought in the Korean War).

Right: It has often been remarked that the Supermarine Attacker was not much more than a jet-powered Spiteful/Seafang, and there is more than a grain of truth in this assertion. The wings, for example, were little changed, a fact clearly evident in this photograph of an early Attacker conducting a publicity sortie for the manufacturer's cameraman.

Like the piston engine, the jet has been with us for so long that people talk about it with easy familiarity but, possibly, no real knowledge. They know that it powers aircraft, that it makes a lot of noise and that it causes vapour trails in the sky, but not too many of those who use the jet actually know how it works. Here, therefore, is a very elementary and brief description of the type of engine produced to power the Attacker—the Rolls-Royce Nene centrifugal-flow turbojet.

The Nene's ancestor was the original jet invented by Air Commodore Sir Frank Whittle in 1941 and the centrifugal design concept was used to power all the first-generation British military aircraft, for example the Vampire, the Meteor, the Sea Venom and the Attacker. It also, in its 'pirated' form, powered the Soviet MiG-15. It had one moving part, a single-drive shaft, to which was attached, at the front, a compressor fan and, at the rear, a disc of turbine blades. The compressor fan-blades were so shaped that they not only increased the pressure of the incoming air from the engine intakes but also threw it out to the periphery of the fan—hence the term 'centrifugal'. From there it was forced into a series of combustion chambers, slightly tapered cylinders clustered lengthwise around the main shaft. Fuel was injected into each chamber, the resultant air/fuel mixture ignited and expanded enormously, and this gas, under high pressure and high velocity, was directed out of the chambers and through the turbine blades at the rear of the drive shaft, thereby powering the compressor fan. The gas exited through the jetpipe, producing the thrust that drove the aircraft.

The engine was normally started up by means of an electric motor, and, at a certain rotor speed,

Above and below: Two photographs of WA497, a production (but here unarmed) Attacker F. Mk 1, prior to its receipt by the Fleet Air Arm. By 1951, when this aircraft made its first flight, a number of modifications to the airframe had been incorporated, most notably the addition of a streamlined fillet at the base of the tailfin; later on, additional grilles and intakes appeared around the tail surfaces.

Opposite: A further change in shape came with the addition of a detachable belly tank, which effectively doubled the aircraft's original fuel capacity. Here, too, can be seen the retractable cockpit access step: boarding the Attacker was still accomplished in the traditional way—stepping up on to the wing trailing edge (avoiding the flap, of course) and proceeding along the wing root.

valves were opened to admit the fuel. At the same time electrical plugs in selected chambers were energised to ignite the mixture, but very quickly ignition spread to all chambers, the combustion process became self-sustaining and the plugs were switched off. They could, however, be used to re-light the engine in flight.

In those early days, engine thrust was measured in four figures. The Nene, for example, developed just over 5,000 pounds. Compare that with the four Rolls-Royce RB.211 engines on Boeing 747s, which each produce 120,000 pounds of thrust! This article is not a technical treatise on the Attacker, but it is for note that access to the engine bay was from the top, and this arrangement was possibly one of the most tedious ever presented to the technicians of the Fleet Air Arm. The cover was an integral part of the aircraft (see the photographs of Pakistani Attackers at the end of this book) and so had to be secured firmly enough to the airframe to take the stresses and strains imposed by high-G flying. This was achieved by securing it to the frame by means of over ninety stubby grub screws—and all this before the days of the electric screwdriver.

When the Attacker F. Mk l finally entered squadron service in 1951—800 Naval Air Squadron was commissioned in August that year—it represented an enormous leap forward, the size of which was not really appreciated until the whole development programme was, as it were, in 'mid-spring'. As in any other branch of research, the unexpected kept cropping up and had to be rectified, designed out of the prototype or incorporated as an advantage. This, one might remark, is what test pilots are for, but the whole involved a wealth of flying experience and a lot of risk—indeed, several lives were lost—before the first squadron of eight aircraft was formed.

800 Squadron was followed by 803 in November 1951 and, finally, by 890 Squadron in April 1952, and it was to this last that I was appointed at the Naval Air Station at Ford, having passed through the flying training pipeline and then been 'fed back' into the Jet Conversion Squadron, 702 NAS, at RNAS Culdrose. It had been rumoured at one time that it was thought that only experienced, second-tour pilots could handle this new and 'formidable' aircraft, and indeed the initial aircrew of 800 Squadron all had that experience, but whether the rumour were true or false, practical common sense prevailed and both 803 and 890 Squadrons had their quota of 'sprog' pilots, none of whom killed themselves. Thereafter it was only a matter of months before 736 Squadron was equipped with Attackers and jet conversion became part of the Fleet Air Arm's standard training pipeline rather than an 'add-on' feature at the end of it.

FROM THE COCKPIT

Commander Graeme Rowan-Thomson

SO it was that, on 24 April 1952, I found myself wandering around a Supermarine Attacker, girding myself up mentally for my first 'fam' in the Navy's first front-line jet fighter, Pilot's Notes in hand and wishing that I had paid more attention to the pre-flight briefing we had all received in the crew room from a pilot assigned to 800 Squadron. The aircraft looked friendly enough. Perhaps it was the straight wing and tail-down attitude—both part of my flying training—that made it so. It certainly didn't have that menacing and aggressive look of the Scimitar and others of the later, swept-wing generation.

The cockpit was sufficiently roomy—just, although there was some discussion as to whether a long-legged pilot would or would not lose his left kneecap on the E.2 standby magnetic compass as he ejected—and there were not too many unfamiliar knobs and levers around. Ah! Wing fold lever! This would be the first time I had flown an aircraft that could actually fold its wings, although in the case of the Attacker the effect was derisory, the span being reduced by a mere two or three feet at the end of each mainplane. During prototype test flying at Supermarine, the pilot, Les Colquhoun, had the starboard wing fold on him in flight. Using full port rudder, he had kept the aircraft straight and, flying as wide a left-hand circuit as possible, managed to land the aircraft at about 200 knots and stop it on the runway—a remarkable feat of skilled flying for which he was awarded the George Medal.

It is always a good idea to get to know where the emergency knobs and levers are in a strange cockpit. A pilot should be able to put his hand on them without hesitation and, conversely, keep his hands away from them when he is not thinking. There was never this problem with the Attacker emergency undercarriage release: well out of sight to the rear of

Below: WA469 was the first production Supermarine Attacker and spent its active career shuttling between the manufacturers and the Aeroplane & Armament Experimental Establishment at Boscombe Down, undergoing a continuing programme of trials and testing.
Right: The main instrument panel of an early Attacker. Compared with front-line aircraft, the piece of equipment most obviously absent is the Gyro Gun Sight immediately in front of the windscreen.

SPECIFICATIONS
SUPERMARINE ATTACKER Mks 1 and 2

Manufacturer:	Supermarine Aircraft Company. Production line at South Marston, Swindon, Wiltshire, and test-flying at Chilbolton, Hampshire.
Design:	Supermarine Type 392 (prototype), Type 398 (production Attacker).
Chief Designer:	Joseph Smith FRAeS.
Powerplant:	One Rolls-Royce Nene 3 turbojet developing 5,000lb (2,270kg, 22.24kN) static thrust.
Dimensions:	Length overall 37ft 1in (11.33m) tail down; wing span 36ft 11in (11.25m) spread, 28ft 11in (8.81m) folded; height 9ft 6½in (3.28m); wing area 227.2 sq ft (21.11m^2).
Weights:	8,426lb (3,820kg) tare, 12,210lb (5,540kg) loaded.
Armament:	Four fixed 20mm Hispano cannon; max. external load (F.B.1 and 2) 2,000lb (900kg) approx.
Performance:	Max. speed 512 kts (590mph, 950kph, Mach 0.73) at sea level; max. climb rate (clean) 6,350ft/min. (1,935m/min.) at sea level; best time to 30,000ft (9,150m) (clean) 6½min.; service ceiling 45,000ft (13,700m).
Number built:	185 (inc. prototypes and export aircraft).

the right cockpit wall, it was hardly a target for impulsive gestures.

One of the biggest innovations was the introduction into RN service of the Martin Baker ejection seat, a wonderful piece of life-saving equipment brought about by the need to give the pilot a means of escape from very high-speed aircraft where the pressure of the slipstream would make it a near impossibility to climb out of the cockpit strapped to a parachute. In the cockpit, the seat was mounted at its rear on to what was really a piston in the barrel of a gun and, in an emergency, the seat, complete with pilot, parachute and dinghy pack, was shot clear of the aircraft by a cordite charge. In the earlier ejection seats there was only a single cordite charge, but the 'g' force this imposed was thought to be too liable to damage the pilot's back and later seats had two charges of lower power, the first starting the seat moving up the 'barrel' and the second firing half way up the travel. In this manner, the acceleration needed for ejection was achieved but in two stages rather than by one hefty kick up the back. The whole process was initiated by the pilot reaching up above his head and pulling down a blind over his face. This activated the 'trigger' of the gun and, at the same time, protected the face from the very considerable force of the slipstream. Once the seat and pilot were clear of the aircraft, a small stabilising parachute was automatically streamed above the seat to stop it tumbling. In the earlier seats the pilot had to release his safety harness, fall out of the seat and deploy his parachute., but the later marks had a barostatic control which automatically released the pilot from the seat below 10,000 feet and deployed the parachute. For high-altitude ejections the pilot was kept in the seat, which had an emergency oxygen supply to keep him conscious whilst he was plunging to lower altitudes. Safety pins had to be inserted in the seat when the aircraft was on the ground to avoid any accidental operation of what was a quite dangerous bit of kit.

Starting the engine required an external power supply from ground batteries, and the procedure was slightly different between the Nene 3 and 102 with regard to when the high-pressure fuel cock was opened. If this was done with too much enthusiasm, the engine would resonate, as the low rpm could not cope with the excess fuel being offered. Following a quick cockpit check, the chocks could be waved away.

Roll forward, a bit of left rudder and squeeze the brake lever to turn left out of dispersal (a differential braking system was fitted)—and the first shock of the trip. The aircraft turned easily enough, but I had to apply opposite brake almost immediately in order to

Left and below: Further views of pre-delivery Attackers. Production was undertaken at Supermarine's South Marston (Swindon) plant, but test-flying had to be carried out at Chilbolton in Hampshire, which had a longer runway. In the photograph below, two aircraft are being checked prior to their first flights; as yet, neither has had its underwing serials applied. Beneath the cockpit is a novel feature—a triangular red warning notice: the Attacker was the first aircraft in the Royal Navy to be equipped with the nowadays mandatory ejection seat, and the symbol drew attention to the explosive nature of this life-saving device. The warning stencilled beneath cautioned against proximity to the intakes when the Nene engine was running.

Left: An aircraft handler checks the elevator as an Attacker pilot carries out his pre-flight procedures in the cockpit prior to a catapult launch on board *Eagle*. The engine is running (as shown by the open auxiliary inlets on the top of the fuselage); the wing flaps are at the take-off setting, but the elevators will be returned to the neutral position (or very slightly nose-up if a belly tank happens to be fitted) prior to departure. This is WA484, an early delivery to 800 Squadron, with, unusually, the undersurface paint colour (Sky Type 'S') carried on the upper surfaces of the fuselage, flanking the tail fin—a template that was abandoned soon after the Attacker entered Fleet Air Arm service.

Above: A 1832 Squadron (Southern Air Division, RNVR) pilot is settled into the cockpit of his aircraft at Benson. Students of markings will note that the 'Royal Navy' legend and serial numbers have been in applied in 'modern' style, in contrast to the stencilled characters more commonly encountered on Attackers.

Below: A late-production Attacker serving with 800 Squadron at Ford. The pilot is about to be strapped in and the trolley accumulator is connected in order to start the engine and systems. The flaps are half down but will raise themselves automatically once the power is on and the engine rotating. The red nose flash seen here first appeared on 800's display aircraft.

control the turn, otherwise the machine would spin on one wheel in a manner that would arouse the professional envy of a ballet dancer. The reason was that the Attacker carried more weight behind the main wheels than her piston-engined equivalents, and therefore possessed more momentum in the turn, allied to the fact that her tail wheel was really two wheels in tandem which pivoted very readily. These latter had to be locked for take-off and landing.

On the runway (with tail wheel locked), I opened up smoothly to full power, and then I realised that I had 5,000 pounds of thrust pushing me forward with increasing vigour. There was no tendency to the swing one experienced in a piston aircraft (caused by the torque of the propeller and also the airflow from it over the fuselage). The tail wheel was raised at 60

knots and I lifted the aircraft easily off the ground at about 105. I prepared to raise the undercarriage and sail away into the blue at the correct climbing speed. That was what was *meant* to happen, but the reality was rather different: everything occurred so much faster than in the piston-powered, tail-wheel aircraft and I found myself desperately trying to catch up with my aeroplane, leaning forward to press the undercarriage 'Up' button and finding the countryside beneath unfolding at an ever-increasing speed—and getting much closer whilst doing so! I tried closing the throttle to climbing power and stopped pressing forward on the stick; I pulled it back, in fact. All this worked and sanity prevailed.

There was a lot of noise, but it was a rumble rather than a roar and then—another 'first' for me—I switched on the cockpit pressurisation. The seals around the cockpit hood expanded and the noise reduced. I settled into the climb, aiming to get up to about 15,000 feet, where I could practise some general handling manœuvres (nothing too spectacular at this stage) and get to feel at home with the aircraft. She did not have powered controls—these came along with the Attacker's successor, the Sea Hawk—so the 'feedback' was entirely natural and what one might expect. The faster I went the heavier the controls felt, and the counter to this was the higher I went the lighter the feel. At height, say 30,000 feet, the controls were light and effective for straight and level flight although they became heavier at high Mach numbers.

The Mach number, so familiar nowadays, was a new speed measurement that pilots had to deal with. The old air speed indicator measured the slipstream air pressure caused by the forward motion of the aircraft but, as the pilot flew higher and maintained his speed, the outside air pressure decreased and therefore his indicated air speed dropped. This did not matter at the lower end of the speed range (the indicated stalling speed was still the same, for example), but it became highly significant in the modern jet, the flight envelope of which was rapidly approaching the speed of sound—the 'sound barrier' of fact and fable. Hence it became necessary to measure the aircraft's true (actual) airspeed relative to the speed of sound at that altitude. In simple language this was done by combining an altimeter with an ASI and calibrating the dial readings as a ratio of the speed of sound—Mach 0.7, 0.8, 1.0 etc. The instrument lacked scientific precision, but it was

Above: WA485 was an unarmed Attacker used in trials work but in October 1951 was lost when it inexplicably dived into the ground during handling tests from Chilbolton, killing its pilot, Lieutenant-Commander Orr-Ewing.

certainly accurate enough to keep the average pilot out of trouble. Today, pilots fly through the sound barrier with as much ease and familiarity as they would go through a swing-door, but in 1952 the RN had no aircraft in service that would do the trick (the swept-wing generation were only just on the horizon), so when I did my first high-speed run in an Attacker I took the whole thing very seriously. The limiting Mach for the aircraft was 0.82, and that could only be reached in a steep dive from height.

I duly climbed up to 35,000 feet, with the aircraft wallowing a bit in the thin air, tested the dive brakes . . . and nearly stalled in the process as my speed suddenly fell away. I put on full power and went into a steep dive. There were two ways of doing this. One was to push the stick forward, which immediately transformed the pilot into a state of negative 'g' and caused every bit of dust and débris to shoot up from the cockpit floor. He was pushed up from his seat and his forward pressure on the stick slackened, so much so that the steep dive became a gentle bunt and he had no chance of achieving 0.82 as he lost height and entered the denser atmosphere. The other, much more effective way was to roll over on to the back, pull back on the stick until the nose seemed to be pointing vertically downwards and then roll the right way up. This had the virtue of positive 'g' throughout the manœuvre and getting the pilot quickly into a steep dive, for without that dive the Attacker stood no chance of hitting its limiting Mach number.

As the speed increased, the controls stiffened markedly (though not beyond the strength of the pilot) and the noise level increased; otherwise there was nothing very dramatic. The excitement came if the pilot tried to recover from this full-power dive by closing the throttle too quickly, in which condition the engine could not ingest the air, resulting in a burbling around the intakes and the aircraft yawing. The best way to counter this was to use the dive brakes: these were highly effective, with just a slight undulation, porpoising, as they went out.

Time to return to base. I had a rough idea of my position but I was in cloud, so I called up my base to ask for a homing and controlled descent. They acknowledged and put me over to the homing frequency, where I was given a 'steer', aiming to get

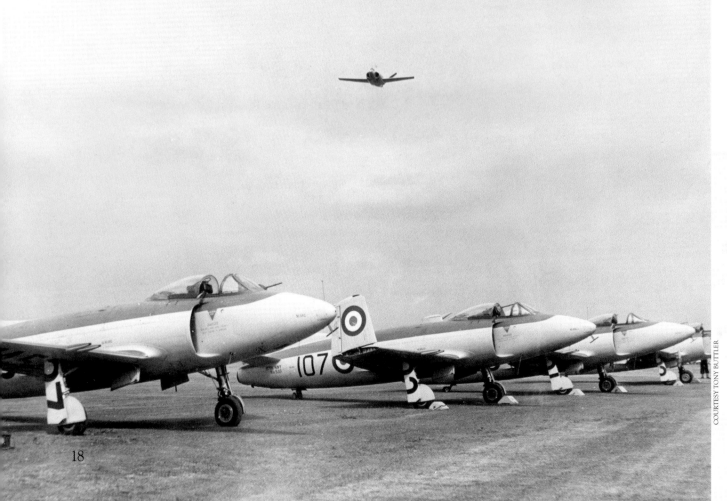

Left, upper: WA497 once more, prior to its delivery to the Fleet Air Arm. The aircraft is unarmed, the four 20mm cannon barrels replaced by aerodynamic stubs.
Left, lower: 800 Squadron about the time of the SBAC Farnborough Air Show in September 1952, with Supermarine's butterfly-tailed Type 529 experimental jet passing overhead. As explained later in the section entitled 'Front-Line Squadrons', Attacker call-signs were not necessarily conclusive clues as to the identity of the establishment to which an aircraft was issued.
Above: Early deliveries to 800 Squadron at Ford, summer 1951. The nose panels covering the attachment points for the ground accumulator cables have been eased away; the third aircraft in line is manned and its Nene is about to be fired up.

me overhead before directing me to let down. In the near future the ground controller would have radar and he would fix my position and feed me into the let-down pattern without having to get me overhead, but that network was not yet in place. Once overhead, I was given a safe bearing and told to 'commence your fast rate of descent'. This plunge down from height was a common feature with jets, but the first time I carried it out it through cloud I had to concentrate very earnestly on my flight instruments: they alone could tell me what the aircraft was doing. I was flying through fog, my eyes were useless, and the forces acting on my body could give very false illusions. I was brought below cloud and in sight of the airfield, so I left the homing frequency and went to the local airfield frequency to join the circuit and land.

This was my first flight in a new aircraft, so my circuit was probably larger than it should have been. I flew downwind with the duty runway on my port side and carried out my 'vital actions'. These took the form of a simple list of checks to help assure a successful landing—undercarriage down and tail wheel locked, flaps selected, wheel brakes on and off again, sufficient fuel for an overshoot, and other requirements peculiar to the type of aircraft. This was not some bureaucratic wish-list: experience had shown that pilots who forget to check these points can crash, sometimes fatally, as a result.

I turned on to the final approach at about 140 knots and let the speed bleed off so that I crossed the airfield boundary at about 105 knots. The aircraft was easy to land in a three-point attitude, although I remembered that when I closed the throttle the deceleration was not as marked as in a propeller-driven machine.

Back on Mother Earth, safe and sound after my first solo on type! It only remained for me to jump out of the cockpit and break my ankle!

TRIALS AND TESTING

TRADITIONALLY, the process of testing new aircraft types destined for front-line service takes the form of two distinct stages. Put very simply, the raw prototype (or prototypes) are delivered to specialist organisations, which in the post-World War II era meant the Aeroplane & Armament Experimental Establishment and the Royal Aircraft Establishment, where hand-picked, highly skilled and experienced staff are charged with assessing the aircraft, reporting their findings and making recommendations concerning improvements and modifications. Once the design's general

Main image: The first prototype displays its undersides.
Below: Flight trials and other forms of examination of aircraft prototypes usually bring about modifications before the design is committed to service, and more often than not these are concerned with 'fine-tuning'. In the case of the Attacker, among the subtle changes introduced between trials and service acceptance were a re-contouring of the main intakes, as seen here is a side-by-side comparison of TS409, the first prototype, and one of the 'WA' series of production aircraft.

'A' and 'C' SQUADRONS, AEROPLANE & ARMAMENT EXPERIMENTAL ESTABLISHMENT

Located at Boscombe Down, Wiltshire

Commanding Officers, 'C' Squadron
Capt. E. M. A. Torrens-Spence DSO DFC AFC*, Cdr D. H. Robertson AFC (00/00/45), Rear-Adm. J. A. Ievers CB OBE (00/00/46), Cdr L. G. Kiggell DSC (00/00/48), Cdr G. R Callingham (00/00/50), Cdr D. B. Law OBE DSC (00/00/52), Cdr S. G. Orr DSC AFC (00/00/54)

ROYAL AIRCRAFT ESTABLISHMENT

Located at Farnborough, Hampshire

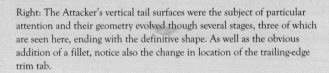

Right: The Attacker's vertical tail surfaces were the subject of particular attention and their geometry evolved though several stages, three of which are seen here, ending with the definitive shape. As well as the obvious addition of a fillet, notice also the change in location of the trailing-edge trim tab.

characteristics have been pronounced acceptable, further examples are issued to service trials establishments so that the type can be 'groomed' into a fully effective combat machine.

Development work does not, of course, stop once the aircraft reaches the front line: there is a programme of continuing improvement as modifications are introduced, new weapon systems appear and, perhaps, new tasks are imposed on the airframe, and this programme will remain in place until the type is rendered obsolete and surplus to requirements. Attackers were flown by the A&AEE and RAE from the time the prototypes first appeared until the mid-1950s and by the service trials and development units, 787 and 703 Naval Air Squadrons, from 1951 until that time.—R.D.C.

A Grave Danger of Floating
Captain Eric Brown CBE DSC AFC

The second prototype Attacker TS413 made its first flight in the hands of Mike Lithgow on 17 June 1947. Shortly afterwards it went to Boscombe Down before coming to RAE, where I first flew it on 2 September. My task included a deck-landing assessment, stability and control tests, and arresting proofing. The aircraft was at an AUW of 11,030 pounds, with the CG at 1.5 inches aft of the datum. The Nene turbojet unit gave 5,000 pounds of static thrust. To my mind the Attacker was not a particularly good-looking aeroplane, being both bulky and angular, and it just did not seem right to be fitted with a conventional tailwheel undercarriage in the new era of the tricycle jet.

On getting into the cockpit I found the view directly ahead and on each beam to be good, but only if I raised myself until my head was touching the top of the canopy, for the front windscreen was not deep enough to provide sufficient field of vision from any other eye level. Furthermore, the seat was too low in the cockpit for me to achieve the desired position when wearing a parachute.

Taxying with the tailwheel free was tricky in that once any turn was initiated it seemed to develop rapidly with the wide-track undercarriage, and harsh braking was required to counteract it. However, with the tailwheel locked taxying was greatly simplified, and turns up to 45 degrees could easily be made under these conditions without any apparent dragging effect being felt from the rear end of the aircraft. Rudder effect alone was useless during taxying, but weathercocking tendencies in a crosswind were only small. For take-off the brakes would only hold the aircraft up to 10,000rpm before they started to slip, but from that point the engine could instantaneously be opened up to the full 12,350rpm without any adverse effects on jet-pipe temperature. There was of course no tendency to swing with the tail wheel lock engaged, but it was not very easy to raise the tail off the ground until the aircraft was almost airborne. However, the view was good, and using take-off flap the run was short. The change of trim on raising the undercarriage was negligible, but raising the flaps gave a very strong nose-

down pitch. By using neutral elevator trim for take-off, the stick force to take up this change of trim was greatly eased.

The Attacker carried almost 300 gallons of fuel and so the stalling speed varied considerably with the reduction in fuel load, but the characteristics were mild. The all-up stall occurred with practically no warning other than a slight twitch on the port aileron about one or two knots before the nose dropped, and the port wing dropped about 15 degrees. The all-down stall was similar, but a slight airframe vibration could be felt a few knots before the port aileron twitch. The only effect of the spoilers on the stall was to increase the airframe vibration to a definite juddering and to add some three knots to the stalling speed. The stalling speeds varied by five knots between a 250-gallon and a 50-gallon fuel load. With the latter load these speeds were 101 knots (all-up), 91 knots (all-down) and 94 knots (all-down, spoilers open).

In cruising flight the controls were well harmonised and effective. Stability was neutral both longitudinally and directionally, but unstable laterally, thus making instrument flying hard work. The aircraft also suffered from directional snaking in any form of turbulence, which would affect its performance as a gun platform. The spoilers had no apparent effect on control up to their limiting speed of 150 knots. They gave the impression of a slight nose-down pitch if opened above 110 knots, but this was merely a deceleration effect felt on the pilot. With a maximum speed of 590mph at sea level, and a maximum rate of climb of 6,350ft/min, the Attacker was a useful performer.

The airfield landing characteristics of the Attacker were really excellent, but it was a different matter for deck-landing owing to a lack of sufficient drag in the landing condition. A final approach at any speed above 1.05Vs (spoilers in) would not give an instantaneous touch-down even when the spoilers were opened at the last moment, so there was a grave danger of floating over all the arrester wires or picking up a wire on the float and being pitched heavily on to the deck, although the long-stroke undercarriage gave a low rebound and therefore damage was unlikely to result from an airborne arrest.

In order to get the best results I evolved the constant power/constant angle approach. On turning in at 115 knots, and assuming 200 gallons of fuel remaining, I set the engine at 8,000rpm and settled on to finals at 110 knots,

Opposite page and above: Three prototype E.10/44 aircraft were ordered in the late summer of 1944 and the first of these, TS409, was flown for the first time by Supermarine test pilot Jeffrey Quill on 27 July 1946; the following year the type was officially named 'Attacker'.

Below: The second prototype, TS413, differed from the first in a number of respects, not least in that it was 'navalised'. It was also equipped with an ejection seat, and featured numerous changes in the shape and area of its control surfaces.

and regulated the approach angle by the spoilers until settled 'in the groove' at 105 knots, when I closed the spoilers and eased back on the stick to reduce speed to 100 knots for the last 50 feet, finally opening the spoilers fully and easing further back on the stick for touch-down. The only effect of picking up an arrester wire with power on was estimated to be a slightly longer pull-out of the wire, but there was no build-up in deceleration. In the event of a baulked landing, full power could be applied instantaneously but gave a strong nose-up trim change which was dangerous at such low speed, but if only 10,000rpm were applied the aircraft would climb away slowly without much change in longitudinal trim.

After this unfavourable deck-landing assessment I started the arresting proofing of the Attacker on the RAE arrester gear on 11 September, and this ended with the arrester hook V-frame being torn out of the aircraft at 3g and the aeroplane being swung violently to port off the runway, though fortunately without further damage. The next day I flew it to Chilbolton airfield for repair. TS413 returned with a strengthened hook three days later and the first stage of arresting proofing was satisfactorily completed this time. Supermarine certainly did not let the grass grow under their feet!

The Ministry of Aircraft Production called a meeting on 18 September at Boscombe Down to review progress to date. At this meeting there were A&AEE pilots and Supermarine's Jeffrey Quill and Mike Lithgow, in addition to those who had been at the first meeting in 1946. The outcome was a decision to increase spoiler travel by 30 per cent and to measure its effect on the baulked landing case with the spoilers open.

The spoiler modification was made with the usual Supermarine speed of action, and I flew the Attacker for assessment on 23 September. The increased travel had increased stalling speed by one knot and gave a marked buffet near the stall. Rate of sink with full spoiler had also increased considerably, so the right effects had been produced. Unfortunately, however, when flying the aircraft at high cruise speed the spoilers got partially and unevenly sucked out of the wing because suction was still present over the spoilers behind the transition point of flow over the laminar flow wing. This caused the aeroplane to roll smartly and resulted in slight distortion damage to the spoilers. However, we were soon back in business and the next flight I made, on 26 September, was to assess the efficiency of the spoilers on touch-down. They now gave a much more positive contact on opening at 1.05Vs, and even at 1.1Vs. It was also clear that, by leaving 8,000 rpm on the engine at touch-down, an immediate getaway on a baulked landing was possible by closing the spoilers first and then opening the throttle.

On 30 September and 1 October, I finished off the arresting proofing with runs up to 3.35g on centre and 2.9g at 15 feet off centre. It is interesting that the tail came up above the horizontal on catching a wire.

On 2 October MAP held a final meeting at Boscombe Down, at which it was agreed that the deck landing trials should go ahead on *HMS Illustrious*. The first deck landing of the Attacker was made by Mike Lithgow on 15 October off the Isle of Wight. This was done at the specific request of Supermarine for publicity reasons and was a break with the normal routine of naval test pilots doing the initial landings. However, Mike was an ex-naval pilot, so it was not an unreasonable request. After landing he handed the Attacker over to me for the first take-off and subsequent landing. The trials involved a total of twelve landings on two days, carried out by an RAE, Supermarine and A&AEE pilot. Only three landings were made on the first day, as it was found that during a tail-first

Main image: Lieutenant-Commander Eric Brown, of the Royal Aircraft Establishment at Farnborough, makes the first take-off in an Attacker prototype from a carrier flight deck: HMS Illustrious, 14 October 1947. These early trials—during which the aircraft was also flown by Supermarine Chief Test Pilot Mike Lithgow (who made the first landing on board) and Lieutenant-Commander Stan Orr of the A&AEE—were preceded by a programme of Aerodrome Dummy Deck Landings (ADDLs) at RNAS Ford.

ATTACKER

Left, upper: Technicians, members of the ship's company and others gather around TS413 following Mike Lithgow's first landing on board HMS *Illustrious*.
Left, lower: The same aircraft caught on camera on a take-off run from the carrier. All the departures conducted during the programme were free take-offs; catapult launches would be investigated on later trials.
Above: While with the A&AEE, TS409 was also taken to the deck, again that of HMS *Illustrious*, but not before early 1950, by which time it had received the standard Fleet Air Arm paint finish.
Below: WA471 (foreground) was another hard-working Attacker. It spent most of its time at Farnborough with the RAE and, amongst other tasks, performed valuable service preparing the way for the introduction of the angled deck. The first prototype is parked alongside it.

touch-down the tailwheel oleo did not absorb the vertical energy imposed on it, the resultant rebound threw the aircraft fuselage into an almost horizontal attitude and unless a wire had been picked up at the point of contact the arrester hook rode above the next few wires until the tail started to drop again. The aircraft was therefore flown back to Chilbolton and Supermarine increased the energy absorption qualities of the tailwheel by 20 per cent, and increased the angle of trail of the hook so that it was some two inches lower than in the original condition.

The trials recommenced on 28 October, and on my four landings I sought progressively to step up the approach speed to test the effectiveness of the spoilers. In fact, these proved to be very effective, but the pilots criticised having to operate a separate spoiler control in addition to the throttle. This moved Supermarine to abandon the spoilers and seek more drag effect by the simple use of drag-producing air brakes. Other, later modifications included a dorsal fin to obviate rudder overbalance propensities, especially when fitted with an external long range tank; flat-sided elevators; and lighter aileron controls.

The first production Attacker was flown on 5 May 1950, and the first squadron formed on 17 August 1951. Thus the Attacker had the distinction of being the Royal Navy's first operational jet aircraft, and for that, if for little else, it will always be remembered.

ATTACKER

Above:

Left: The work of the A&AEE and the RAE on the Attacker did not end when the aircraft entered service: it continued throughout its career with the Fleet Air Arm. WK319, the first F.B. Mk 2, was heavily involved in work at both establishments, and is seen here on board HMS Eagle undergoing catapult trials while carrying mock-up R/Ps. The aircraft is not about to launch: the wings are folded, take-off flap is yet to be selected, the stops are still raised, the wheel chocks are still in place and the catapult bridle has yet to be positioned (note the shuttle in the left foreground and the strop lying between the mainwheels). The steam streamer, forward, gives an indication of wind strength and direction.

Above: WA469, the first production Attacker, was in the hands of the A&AEE for most of its career. This was the aircraft that Les Colquhoun was flying when he had a mishap that culminated in an amazing feat of airmanship for which he was deservedly awarded the George Medal—as described by the author on page 10 and by Commander 'Mike' Crosley on page 38.
Below: Rocket-Assisted Take-Off Gear (RATOG) was developed during World War II and was available for many years thereafter to most front-line naval aircraft should a shorter (or speedier) take-off than normal be called for. The third prototype, seen here, was among those aircraft that tested the installation on the Attacker, in the hands of the RAE at Farnborough.

"ATTACKER" AIRCRAFT EMERGENCY LANDING 28th OCT. 1949
30 RUNWAY
DUMMY RUN

30 RUNWAY

RUNWAY 25
RUNWAY 30

Left: A sequence of photographs showing the adventure that befell the A&AEE's Lieutenant-Commander G. F. Hawkes in TS409, the original Attacker prototype, on 28 October 1949. Tasked with conducting deck-landing trials on board HMS *Illustrious*, he was about to begin when he discovered that the starboard undercarriage leg would not lock down.

Sensibly electing to try his luck at the more extensive—and somewhat softer—acreage offered by RNAS Culdrose, he managed to carry out a first-rate forced landing.

Above: Lieutenant-Commander Hawkes emerges from his aircraft, to general relief all round.

Above: WA535 served with the A&AEE at Boscombe Down in 1952 on connection with elevator trials before being transferred to 767 Squadron.

Right: Not precisely an Attacker but in general terms a swept-wing version of it, the experimental Supermarine Type 510 was to provide valuable experience to the manufacturers, the RAE and the A&AEE and was an important stage in the development of the Swift and Scimitar fighters. VV106 is seen here in the landing configuration.

No Hanging About
Lieutenant-Commander Don Moore-Searson

TOWARDS the end of 1950, after some eighteen months instructing at Lossiemouth in the Naval Operational Flying School where, as a QFI (Qualified Flying Instructor), I had been flying Fireflies and Seafires, I decided that the time had come for me to make tentative inquiries about what my next appointment might be. My thoughts were that, having had the good fortune to fly a Vampire Mk 3 whilst I was learning to be an instructor at the Central Flying School, I should aim to be amongst the first Fleet Air Arm pilots to fly the new generation of naval jet fighters that were then being developed. So, having discussed the matter with the Appointer at the Admiralty, the die was cast. Within days I was on my way to 702 Squadron at RNAS Culdrose to make my acquaintance with the Meteor T.7 and the Sea Vampire on what was then called the Long Jet Course.

Three weeks later I joined 787 Squadron, the Naval Air Fighting Development Unit (NAFDU), based at RAF West Raynham in Norfolk. Here, with a number of other new arrivals to the jet world, we were tasked first to investigate and develop suitable methods for the tactical operation of jet aircraft from aircraft carriers and then to carry out an intensive flying trial with the first of the new Supermarine Attackers.

At that time it was realised that the introduction of jet fighters to naval aviation posed a number of problems. There was, for instance, considerable concern about the very high rate of fuel consumption in jet aircraft compared with piston aircraft. This meant that there could be no hanging about on the ground or flight deck after the engines had been started as jets had to be quickly launched into a climb to high altitude, where they would be able to operate to their maximum efficiency. Similarly, at the conclusion of a mission, jets had to be swiftly recovered into the landing pattern and back on the deck lest any of the aircraft run out of fuel.

It was a completely new situation. Little of the existing practice—flying circuits at low altitude, without too much concern for fuel consumption—could be retained. Ways had to be found to keep jets safely at a high altitude for as long as possible, and then to recover them expeditiously to the deck with the minimum expenditure of fuel. For example, the tedious 'wall of death', forming up and circling at 300 feet whilst waiting for a large number of aircraft to join, could no longer be tolerated. The carriers had to be able to land-on all the jet aircraft at the end of a sortie when only some four or five minutes or so of the last aircraft's fuel remained, and to achieve this the waiting area, for aircraft at the conclusion of a sortie, had to be moved up to a minimum of 20,000 feet in the vicinity of the carrier. This meant that jet aircraft would invariably be above cloud and out of sight of the carrier, and the Fighter Direction Officers in the carrier had to be trained to work closely with the squadron pilots so that they were able to understand the technical problems involved in flying jet aircraft.

Whilst awaiting the arrival of the Attackers we used Vampire 5s to work out the various techniques. We also had our own Fighter Direction Officer appointed to operate with us and we very soon achieved a close working relationship with him. This was extremely important, as operating a squadron of aircraft to the limits of the latter's manoeuvrability and endurance meant that information between aircraft and the director had to be passed rapidly and with the minimum amount of speech. We and our director soon developed a crisp jargon to exchange vital data, and, as I was to find out later, when it came to a question of confidence in what we were being asked to carry out, it was vital to be able to recognise the voice of the person we were talking to.

The first Attacker arrived in April 1951 and was closely followed by a second and then a third. These aircraft were fitted with ejection seats, equipment that was very new to us, and we all had to go along to Martin Baker to be briefed by Bernard Lynch about how to use them and to gain some idea of what it was all about by being strapped into a seat and then fired up the ramp in the test rig they had built at Denham. This rig was rather like a rail track inclined backwards at about thirty degrees and about forty feet high along which the seat would travel when the ejection sequence was activated. It was, indeed, quite an experience: one moment you would be sitting in the seat chatting to the various people standing around and then, on the word 'eject,' you would pull the face blind, there was a muffled explosion from behind and, suddenly, you would find

787 NAVAL AIR SQUADRON
Naval Air Fighting Development Unit
Located at RAF West Raynham, Norfolk

Commission
09/04/45–17/08/55 (Attacker F.1s 00/01/51–00/04/52, F.B.1s 00/09/54–00/09/54, F.B.2s 00/04/54–00/09/54)

Commanding Officer(s)
Lt-Cdr B. H. C. Nation, Lt-Cdr W. I. Campbell (04/09/51), Lt-Cdr S. G. Orr DSC AFC (04/03/53), Lt-Cdr R. E. Bourke (08/10/53), Lt-Cdr R. D. Taylor (01/01/54), Lt-Cdr R. A. Shilcock (24/07/54)

Senior Pilot(s)
Not known

ROYAL NAVAL HANDLING SQUADRON
Located at RAF Manby, Lincolnshire

Commanding Officer (No 4 Squadron RAF)
Sqn Ldr L. J. Roxburgh RAF (in 1953)

RN Officer-in-Charge
Lt-Cdr R. M. Crosley DSC* (in 1953)

TRIALS AND TESTING

Right: The Naval Air Fighting Development Unit (NAFDU) was co-located, and shared many facilities, with the Royal Air Force's Air Fighting Development Squadron (itself a component of the Central Fighter Establishment). Its task was to conduct specialised trials of newly introduced FAA aircraft, with the emphasis on developing combat techniques. A number of Attackers were employed by the Unit during the course of the aircraft's service career, including the early-production WA486 shown here in what appears to be a retouched photograph. Lieutenant-Commander Don Moore-Searson writes on these pages of his experiences whilst serving with the Unit. The Royal Naval Handling Squadron, about which Commander 'Mike' Crosley writes on pages 38–39, was involved principally with testing (to their limits) brand new aircraft types, and subsequent marks thereof, in order to establish the parameters for the compilation of the Pilot's Notes.

yourself swaying gently from side to side at the top of the rig and gazing down at those to whom you had just been talking. We learned that these Mk 1 seats required a minimum of about 4,000 feet of altitude for safe operation because, after ejection, the pilot would still be firmly attached to the seat, which by then would be hurtling downwards, suspended beneath its stabilising drogue. He had then to undo the seat straps and fall out of the seat, and after that pull the parachute ripcord manually. There was an additional hazard in the Attacker because, on ejection, the clearance between the pilot's knees and the cockpit coaming was very marginal and there existed the possibility of losing one's kneecaps in the process. Such was the concern about this matter that a test was carried out to determine whether or not some pilots should be excluded from flying the aircraft. So, with the seat unlocked and the ejection cartridges removed, we were kitted up and strapped into the seat whilst a crane pulled it up the cockpit guide rails. In the event, the worst case established that the clearance was of the order of a quarter of an inch between the inside edge of the coaming and the outside of the knees!

I was quite impressed by how well Supermarine had designed the layout of the Attacker's cockpit instrumentation and controls. Everything was where one would expect to find it but, instead of having the old-fashioned spade grip at the top of the control column, the Attacker was fitted with a neat, American-style, moulded hand grip. However, unlike the Vampire and Meteor, the aircraft retained the classic piston-engined tail-wheel undercarriage.

This was complicated by the necessary inconvenience of a tail-wheel lock which one had to remember to set before commencing the take-off run and to release prior to attempting to turn off the runway after landing. Furthermore, contrary to the practice in the Vampire and Meteor, when flying the Attacker the stick had to be initially pushed forward during the take-off run in order to raise the tail.

It was during trials to ascertain how agile the Attacker was in simulated combat that we discovered that its directional stability left a lot to be desired. Any harsh over-correction using the rudder at high speed during entry to or recovery from a steep turn tended to cause the aircraft to flick into a roll. To correct this, Supermarine fitted it with an elongated dorsal fin. The ailerons were, however, very light and gave the Attacker a high rate of roll. Another concern was that the lack of directional stability could result in a severe disturbance to the airflow as it entered the engine intakes on either side of the fuselage. This problem was highlighted when the aircraft being flown by Lieutenant McDermott developed a severe intake banging noise that was quickly followed by a catastrophic engine failure. There was only one thing left for him to do: he was the first pilot to eject from a service aircraft. Meanwhile, as a cure for the intake problem was being developed, the trials programme continued, albeit with extreme care. The remedy was to redesign the profiling of the intakes.

Having been brought up on piston-engined aircraft with their comparatively modest fuel consumption, one was usually able to return to the carrier from a sortie with a

```
ATTACKER PERFORMANCE FIGURES.

1.  CRUISING SPEEDS.
                    11,800 REVS.      FULL
    HEIGHTS.        MAXIMUM           L.R.T.
                    CONTINUOUS.       RANGE.           ENDURANCE.

    10,000'         356 (.62)         250 knts.    ⎫
    15,000'         320               240   "      ⎪
    20,000'         315               235   "      ⎬   180 knts.
    25,000'         300               230   "      ⎪
    30,000'         270               225   "      ⎪
    35,000'         220               220   "      ⎭

2.  TURNING CIRCLES.

    HEIGHTS.        Rate I.           Min. radius.

    10,000'                           .75 mls.   ⎫
    15,000'         2 mls.            .9  mls.   ⎪
    20,000'                           1   ml.    ⎬
    25,000'                           1.2 mls.   ⎪   11,800
    30,000'         2-¼ mls.          1.3 mls.   ⎪
    35,000'                           1.5 mls.   ⎭

3.  LIMITATIONS. (Practical for interceptions)
                                      PRACTICAL SPEEDS
    HEIGHTS.        Mach No.          FOR CRUISING.

    10,000'                           400 I.A.S.  ⎫
    15,000'         .75 ind.          380    "    ⎪
    20,000'                           325    "    ⎬
    25,000'         .78 max.          300    "    ⎪   .7
    30,000'         True .            270    "    ⎪
    35,000'                           235    "    ⎭

                    FUEL STATE.
4.  CLIMBING.       I         II        III
                    FULL      180 gals. No.        Distance Covered
    HEIGHTS.        L.R.T.    L.R.T.    L.R.T.     in still air.
                    Mins.sec. mins.sec. mins.sec.  Miles.
     5,000'          2.45      2.40      2.10          10
    10,000'          4.23      4.15      3.20          20
    15,000'          6.32      6.13      4.48          30
    20,000'          9.23      8.41      6.40          40
    25,000'         12.24     11.34      8.37          50
    30,000'         15.57     14.49     10.53          65
    35,000'         21.04     19.07     14.00          85
    40,000'                             17.47

         Runs have been adjusted
       since these figures were compiled
       Approx 1½ mins. can be taken off
              time to 35,000'

5.  RANGE.

    HEIGHT.         F.L.R.T.          Empty.

    10,000'         600 mls.          275 mls.  ⎫
    15,000'         650  "            295  "    ⎪  This is absolute
    20,000'         700  "            320  "    ⎬  range climbing
    25,000'         750  "            330  "    ⎪  and d scending
    30,000'         840  "            350  "    ⎪  on track.
    35,000'         940  "            375  "    ⎭

6.  ENDURANCE - SAFE.

    Fuel State.              Time.

         I               1 hr. 30 mins.
         II              1 hr. 15 mins.
         III                   45 mins.
```

Left: A facsimile of the data sheet containing the original performance figures for the Supermarine Attacker, as compiled by members of the NAFDU at West Raynham. These are interesting for a number of reasons, not least in how they differ from the information conveyed by most published reports (including the generalised manufacturer's figures, summarised on page 12 of this book!). For example, the figures for the rate of climb indicate that the Attacker was not as swift to altitude as is generally thought; moreover, the rate varied considerably according to the fuel state.

Right: Two further views of WA486, emphasising the Attacker's streamlining and the dihedralled tailplane. The odd angle of the jet efflux rim helped to deflect hot gases away from the ground when the aircraft was starting up and taxying.

reasonable amount of reserve fuel left in the tanks. Now, the introduction to jets was quite an eye-opener: we had to become used to operating them down to the last few gallons remaining. The Attacker's internal fuel system, containing a total of 293 gallons, consisted of six tanks each feeding into a central main collector tank, which had a capacity of 82 gallons. A warning light in the cockpit would indicate when the fuel from the six tanks had finished transferring to the main tank. When this occurred the fuel remaining in the main tank would generally have dropped to about 70 gallons, and we would take this as the signal to start the return to base.

The 250-gallon ventral drop tank, introduced some time later, also fed into the main tank. Fuel transfer to the main tank from either the internal tanks or the drop tank was controlled by a selector lever on the starboard cockpit shelf. When using fuel from the drop tank, a warning light would indicate to the pilot that it had finished transferring and the main tank gauge would start to show a reduction in quantity. The selector lever then had to be moved from its forward position to the aft position in order to allow the transfer of fuel from the internal tanks. Failure of this lever to operate would mean that only the remaining fuel in the main tank was available—an experience I was to enjoy later while serving in 800 Squadron at Ford.

RAF West Raynham, situated on damp, low-lying land not far from the east coast in Norfolk, was, under certain rare meteorological conditions, subject to what is known as

a 'haar'. It tended to occur when a cold, damp wind was coming in from the east, and the airfield and surrounding area would suddenly become enveloped in fog. It was also responsible for a rather traumatic personal experience. On 26 April 1951 I had been programmed to team up with a colleague for an eight o'clock take-off. Early that morning, a glimpse outside at the weather indicated that it was cold and damp, with an overcast of very low, dark grey cloud, and what little wind there was barely stirred the trees. A telephone call to the Met office produced a forecast that we should expect varying amounts of cloud from about 800 feet extending up to about 28,000 feet. Below this, we were told, there was a broken layer of stratus at 400 feet above the airfield. This would be all right, we thought, as our exercises were to be carried out above 30,000 feet, and we could find our way back to the airfield with a QGH approach.

I was in WA482, the second aircraft to start up, and I followed my colleague as we taxied out to take off with a ten-second interval along the main runway heading towards the west. I remembered then, as I penetrated the bottom layer of stratus, that I had not noticed any other aircraft standing in the dispersal: it seemed that ours were to be the only two in the air at that time. The Attacker was, however, quite a nice aircraft to fly on instruments, and very soon the gloomy turbulence of the cloud gave way to brilliant sunshine as the aircraft cleared the top at about 38,000 feet, where I was able to begin the series of tests I had been briefed to carry out—the determining of turning-circle distances covered at various Mach numbers and turn rates. Whilst jotting down the data on my kneepad I heard my colleague in the other Attacker calling over the radio that he was returning to base and requesting a QGH descent. Ten seconds later my fuel transfer warning light came on and I also called for a QGH. One after the other the Controller, using his CRDF (cathode ray direction finding set)—whereby, when the pilot transmitted on his radio a marker appeared on a screen to indicate the bearing of the aircraft from the airfield—directed us to a position overhead the airfield at 30,000 feet. Then he instructed us to turn on to the reciprocal of the runway heading and commence a high-speed descent. At 15,000 feet we were instructed to turn left on to the runway heading and reduce the rate of descent; further heading corrections were given as we approached the airfield. We were then instructed to level off at 400 feet, the lowest safe altitude for a QGH approach.

When I heard my colleague call that he was breaking through the lower level and had the runway in sight, I was still in cloud at 400 feet. I then called to inform the Controller of my predicament and was instructed to 'nudge' the aircraft down to 300 feet. But a quick glance over the side indicated that I was still in cloud. By this time my fuel was down to 35 gallons and so, after I had announced this fact, I called for a GCA, a precision, radar-controlled approach that could get me down to a hundred feet above the runway surface. Unfortunately, as I found out later, the GCA crew were then in the process of changing watches, and as the wind had now gone round to the east the precision approach radar element of the GCA equipment was, of course, pointing the wrong way and, because of this, unable to provide me with any glide slope information.

My call for assistance had come at the wrong time. They were only able to discern my position relative to the airfield and so were restricted to telling me which way to steer and my distance from the runway threshold. I had been directed on to the duty runway threshold at a height of 1,000 feet, and so the final descent to touch-down had to be made by means of a 'step-down' approach, reducing my height above the runway in stages—the aim being to arrive at the threshold at about fifty feet above it and with the runway in sight. The conditions were such that, after two aborted attempts, I had not seen the runway. By then I only had twenty gallons remaining as I overshot the airfield—insufficient fuel to climb high enough for a safe ejection in the Mk 1 seat. In about three minutes all the fuel would have gone and the engine would stop.

There was now no choice but to try for a third GCA. I remember suppressing a brief moment of panic as I realised the near hopelessness of my situation, and then, after saying a very quick prayer I called up for this final attempt. Luckily, as it happened, the Squadron Leader who was in charge of the GCA system was in the control tower at the time and had been monitoring the radio traffic. Aware of the emergency, he rushed over to the GCA site and quickly took charge. Recognising his voice over the radio was an immense help as I settled down to concentrate and carry out the best bit of instrument flying that I had ever done. In a calm voice he guided me round on to the approach heading, informing me that, as there was no glide slope information available, he would be calculating the changes to my height on the final approach in relation to the distance to go to the touch-down position on the runway, and directing me to reduce height as necessary to achieve a three-degree descent path. Knowing that I needed the aircraft to respond rapidly to any control inputs I might wish to make, I increased the final approach speed by five knots to 105. At one hundred feet as indicated on the alti-

meter, a quick glance upwards told me I was still in cloud. Again, at fifty feet there was still no outside visibility. I was also aware that the altimeter, after a soak at high altitude, suffered from hysteresis and could over-read by some sixty feet! The controller continued to talk me in and gave minor corrections to my heading. Eventually, close beside the port wing tip, I briefly caught sight of the glow of a flare through the fog. There was no high-intensity approach lighting at West Raynham at that time, but someone had had the presence of mind to ignite a flare at the side of the runway. Seconds later I felt a bump as the wheels hit the surface.

Unable, because of the fog, to see exactly where I was and because of the excess speed, I realised I had to slow the aircraft as rapidly as possible by retracting the undercarriage. This turned out not to be an easy task as the weight of the aircraft on the 'down' locks prevented the retraction sequence from operating. So, in desperation, I reached down to find the emergency switch that would electrically withdraw the undercarriage down locks. But as this failed to work I jammed on full left brake and then reversed the rudder to full right brake hoping that the resultant violent left and right forces would break the undercarriage locks. This did the trick, as first one undercarriage leg folded and then the other followed, causing the aircraft to lurch from side to side as the fuselage came down into contact with the runway. The aircraft then streaked along on its belly before eventually coming to rest in a field, having penetrating the airfield boundary fence. The obligatory large glass of rum in the Station Sick Bay also worked, leaving me to fill in the subsequent A.25. Several weeks later I received a commendation, which was duly inserted in my log book!

Main image: WA482 at rest following Don Moore-Searson's adventure at RAF West Raynham.
Above: The log book entry, citing 'highly commendable calmness and skill'.

ATTACKER

Checking on the Machery *Commander R. M. ('Mike') Crosley DSC**

The first large order for 80 Attackers had been given by the Admiralty in early 1951. 800 Squadron was the first to embark aboard *Eagle* with the fighter version, where it showed itself to be a good formation-flying and demonstration aircraft but a disappointing fighter plane. The remainder of the eighty Attackers ordered were converted to the fighter-bomber rôle and remained in service until October 1954.

Jeffrey Quill had taken the first prototype Attacker into the air from Boscombe Down on 27 July 1946. Mike Lithgow flew the second prototype from Chilbolton a year later and Les Colquhoun had continued with development testing until it came out of first-line service in June 1954. It was Les Colquhoun who was awarded the George Medal for landing the prototype 'navalised' Attacker after one of its wings had folded in the air, jamming the ailerons. On 23 May 1950 Les had just completed a fast run over the airfield at about 450 knots when he heard a loud bang and on looking out saw the outer three feet six inches of wing standing up vertically. The aircraft still flew on, and, realising that he still had some lateral control due to the positive dihedral effect of the folded portion of the wing compensating for the loss of lift in the starboard wing, he decided to try to control it with rudder and elevator alone (the ailerons having self-locked when the wing folded). Coarse use of rudder was just sufficient to control bank at speeds above 230 knots, so he decided not to bale out. He crossed the airfield boundary at 230 knots, touching down at 200 knots, twice the normal approach speed of the Attacker. He said, 'By juggling with the elevator and brakes to keep the aircraft on the ground I pulled up ten yards short of the end of the 1,800-yard runway.'

As the Attacker, like the Sea Hawk, had the 5,000-pound static thrust Rolls-Royce Nene 3 engine, and as the fighter version of the Attacker weighed only twice this engine thrust, I was expecting it to climb at twice the rate and at twice the speed of a Seafire. This turned out to be too optimistic a guess, even for the first 15,000 feet, and above this height the thrust progressively fell off until at about 30,000 feet it was barely sufficient to keep the airspeed high enough for the steep turns essential for fighter combat. Although faster than the Sea Vampire and a little faster than the Meteor Mk 4, and with a better rate of roll than either with its power-boosted ailerons, the Attacker was not sufficiently far ahead in performance as a fighter by 1952 and it was soon relegated to the fighter-bomber rôle. The FB version which arrived at Manby [where I was conducting my testing] was therefore equipped with bomb racks, a 250-gallon belly tank and rocket launchers. All that was necessary was to find out its fuel consumption, check on its 'Machery' handling, do some landings with bomb and rocket 'hang-ups' and add this information to the current Pilot's Notes for the fighter version.

In a dogfight with a Sabre Mk 4 one day, it was noticeable that the Attacker's controls seemed to be far too heavy for a fighter (after the delights of a Seafire) and above about 15,000 feet it seemed to lack sufficient lift from its laminar-flow, ex-Spiteful wing to out-turn this much faster American fighter—which, having shot the writer down, dived away easily, leaving him to struggle to retain enough elevator control to pull out in time before hitting the ground at a Mach number no higher than about 0.78. It was probably the Attacker's habit of 'tucking its nose down' and not responding to elevator above Mach 0.82 that led to the deaths of 'Spike' King-Joyce and, later, of Lieutenant-Commander Malcolm Orr-Ewing—characteristics which added to its unsuitability as an interceptor fighter. Neither

TRIALS AND TESTING

Above and below: 'The FB version which arrived at Manby was . . . equipped with bomb racks, a 250-gallon belly tank and rocket launchers.' This particular example, WK338, has RATOG fitted also—above and below the wing trailing edges adjacent to the fuselage.

was it as easy to deck-land as the nose-wheeled Sea Vampire. It certainly needed the assistance of the newly invented gyro-stabilised mirror landing sight installed in *Eagle* to allow it to operate from a carrier without too many accidents.

From about March 1953 onwards the Attacker was withdrawn from front-line service in 800 and 803 Squadrons and replaced with the Hawker Sea Hawk F. Mk l, beginning with 800 Squadron. Most of the remaining Attackers were given to 736 (Jet Training) Squadron at Lossiemouth or allotted to three of our excellent RNVR squadrons, 1831, 1832 and 1833. Unfortunately, three years later, on 10 March 1957, and in spite of their magnificent help in the Korean War, all the RNVR squadrons were abolished by the 'Sandys Axe' and their remaining Attackers and other aircraft were transferred to fleet requirements units to provide targets for gunners until their end in 1958.

703 and 700 NAVAL AIR SQUADRONS

Located at RNAS Ford (700 NAS formed out of 703 NAS 18/08/55 on latter's disbandment)

Commissions
703 NAS–19/04/45–17/08/55 (Attacker F.1s 00/07/51–00/08/51, F.B.1s 00/01/52–00/04/52, F.B.2s 00/04/55–17/08/55); 700 NAS–18/08/55–03/07/61 (Attacker F.B.2s 18/08/55–00/02/56)

Commanding Officer(s)
703 NAS–Lt-Cdr J. M. Glazer DSC, Lt-Cdr S. M. Longsden (08/01/53), Lt-Cdr F. J. Sherborne (20/07/53), Lt-Cdr J. R. N. Gardner DSC (04/09/53), Lt-Cdr F. E. Cowtan (14/03/55); 700 NAS–Lt-Cdr R. W. Turral, Lt-Cdr D. G. Halliday (16/01/56)

Senior Pilot(s)
Not known

TRIALS AND TESTING

Above, left and right: Borne out of the Naval Air-Sea Warfare Development Unit, by 1951 703 Squadron had evolved into the Royal Navy's Service Trials Unit, one of the main duties of which was the testing of catapult and arrester gear, not so much on the aircraft it flew as on the carriers from which these aircraft would operate. Thus, when the Attacker entered production for the Fleet Air Arm and it had been decided that the brand new HMS *Eagle* would be the first (and, in the event, the only) carrier to receive on board operational Attacker squadrons, 703 NAS was issued with a small number of aircraft to develop and perfect the techniques required to launch and recover them. Here WA470, an unarmed early production Attacker which was transferred to 703 Squadron from the A&AEE, is seen about to touch down on HMS *Illustrious* in November 1951 during deck-landing trials; notice the droop of the flaps—virtually 90 degrees—and, in the photograph on the right, the DLCO's backscreen and also presence of the faithful plane-guard vessel, ready to aid of the pilot in case of mishap. As recounted in subsequent pages of this book, certain aspects of the trials (notably barrier arrests) had to be undertaken by front-line squadrons owing to delays in the commissioning of *Eagle* and the consequent urgency to get operational squadrons to sea.

Left: HMS *Illustrious*—a familiar sight to Attacker pilots carrying out DLP (Deck-Landing Practice). In the immediate postwar years the task of taking front-line Fleet Air Arm squadrons to sea was carried out, in the main, by the light fleet carriers of the *Majestic* and *Colossus* class and two of the six large fleet carriers of the *Illustrious* class, *Implacable* and *Indomitable*; of the remainder of the latter class, *Indefatigable* and *Illustrious* herself, weary from arduous war service, were employed in the training rôle, *Victorious* was earmarked for major conversion and *Formidable* was regarded as too worn out to be worthy of upgrading. Postwar frugalities had reduced the number of big fleet carriers of the *Audacious* class, still under construction in 1945, to two vessels, *Ark Royal* and *Eagle*—the building of both of which was so seriously delayed by political and financial constraints that neither was ready until the early 1950s.

Left and right: Deck-landing Practice for 803 Squadron pilots took place on board HMS *Illustrious* in March 1952, some two months before embarkation on board HMS *Eagle*. At this time WA527 was being utilised by pilots from both 800 and 803 Squadrons, although it was theoretically assigned to 703 Squadron.

Below: WZ277, a late-production Attacker F.B.2, joined 703 Squadron towards the end of its commission and was transferred to 700 Squadron when the former unit was absorbed by the latter in August 1955. It is seen here, unmarked, at RNAS Ford alongside a Fairey Gannet. Something akin to a bomb trolley appears to have been 'censored' in this photograph.

TRIALS AND TESTING

FRONT-LINE SQUADRONS

Rear-Admiral Ray Rawbone CB DSC

SUPERMARINE test pilot Mike Lithgow carried out the first deck landing of an Attacker on board HMS *Illustrious* in August 1947, but it was not until April 1949 that the first jet evaluation and training unit was set up as 702 Squadron (see page 82 *et seq.*) at RNAS Culdrose. Bruce Clark was the CO, and he was succeeded by 'Pete' Perrett. Its complement of aircraft was initially based on Meteor Mk 7s and Vampire Mk 20s. Its aim was to 'feed' pilots through the Squadron before joining the first operational jet units.

All the instructors were experienced jet pilots, and by 1951 the RN had built up a reasonable 'pool' of such officers ready to join the new Attacker squadrons. I was fortunate enough to have been on loan to the central Flying School for two and a half years and had quite a lot of jet experience, including the award of one of the first jet instrument rating examiner's 'tickets'. With some foresight, George Baldwin ensured that I was appointed to 702 Squadron early enough to help qualify his designated 800 Squadron pilots with instrument rating

cards before the unit formed at RNAS Ford on 21 August 1951.

800 Squadron, under the command of George Baldwin, comprised ten pilots and an engineer officer; we were followed shortly afterwards by 803 Squadron (CO Tommy Handley). Both squadrons were initially equipped with eight Attacker F. Mk 1s, although the establishment of each was increased to twelve aircraft the following year when Attacker F. B. Mk 2s became available from 890 Squadron—a 'pool' established in January 1952 and disbanded some ten months later.

Below: The entire complement of aircraft from 800 and 803 Squadrons—eight in each—parked forward after landing on board HMS *Eagle* in 1952. Wing-folding has long been characteristic of naval aircraft, permitting much more efficient stowage both above and below deck. As can be seen here, even merely turning up the wing tips of the Attacker made all the difference: aircraft could be parked three abreast at the bow instead of two. However, the primary reason for shortening the span in this particular instance was to enable the aircraft to fit *Eagle*'s 33-foot-wide after lift (the forward lift was 44 feet wide) while remaining aligned fore-and-aft. The two catapult tracks can be glimpsed beneath the aircraft. These systems were of the older, hydraulic variety: steam catapults would not arrive on HM aircraft carriers until the commissioning of *Eagle*'s half-sister *Ark Royal* in February 1955.

ATTACKER

The Size of the Biceps *Rear-Admiral Ray Rawbone* CB DSC

We embarked in *Eagle* in March 1952 and the following months were spent operating, alternately, from the carrier and from Ford. Whilst embarked we deployed to the North Sea, the Norwegian Sea and the Mediterranean. The Squadron notched up a British 'first' when we were privileged to take part in 'touch-and-go' trials on an angled deck marked out on the flight deck of the USS *Antietam* operating in the Channel just south of Ford. The trials were very successful, and I am sure that Keith Leppard, our specialist and gallant 'batsman', was one of many who were very happy to anticipate redundancy and the time when they were no longer required to risk life and limb guiding wayward pilots safely on to the flight deck!

At this time, the routines for safe instrument descents through thousands of feet of cloud were in their infancy. We rarely had full radar cover and relied mainly on bearings passed by the carrier or shore base. A flight of four aircraft would home on bearings until overhead the carrier. The flight leader would then continue on a predetermined course for a set period whilst forming up his aircraft *en echelon* port or starboard. The aircraft would break away in turn, at ten-second intervals, on to a set pattern of courses, descending at the same speed and rate of descent until on final approach below cloud. A turn on to each new course was based on the bearings each aircraft received from the carrier during descent. Arrival in the correct order on finals relied on accurate instrument flying, and surprisingly was usually (if not always!) successful in providing about a minute's interval between aircraft on the final approach.

Bruce Clark had a rather erratic No. 4 who was the last to turn into the descent, the last to enter cloud but invariably the first to arrive out of cloud on the final approach to the carrier! We never did find out why, but the climax came one day when Bruce was about three or four hundred yards away from a touch-down on final approach and his No. 4 appeared just ahead and underneath him! 'Flash' was a very popular member of our team, but, wisely, he was reappointed, and survived to be ordained in civilian life.

Most front-line squadrons set up a formation aerobatic team: it enhanced teamwork and boosted morale. 803 and

800 NAVAL AIR SQUADRON

Located at RNAS Ford and on board HMS *Eagle*

Commission
22/08/51–11/06/54 (Attacker F.1s 22/08/51–00/05/52, F.B.1s 00/02/52–00/01/53, F.B.2s 00/09/52–11/06/54)

Commanding Officer(s)
Lt-Cdr G. C. Baldwin DSC*, Lt-Cdr R. W. Kearsley (03/12/52), Lt-Cdr W. I. Campbell (23/12/53)

Senior Pilot(s)
Lt-Cdr D. R. O. Price

800 Squadrons decided to join forces, starting with nine aircraft but later reducing to seven. We performed at Air Days, and of course took part in the Fly Past during the Coronation Review (though not aerobatically, of course). The team of seven pilots was led by the Senior Pilot of 803, Bill MacDonald. We quickly realised that we had to be extremely smooth and careful in our routines because between us we could muster twenty-one children! Bill himself had six, and the weight of parenthood certainly rested heavily upon his shoulders.

Our routines consisted of a combination of loops and rolls. The Attacker was light on the ailerons but very heavy in the looping plane, and it was said that you could always tell an Attacker pilot by the size of his biceps! Because of the time required to turn a tight formation, there were periods of 'dead time'—gaps in the routine when nothing would be happening in front of the spectators—and for this

Left: One of several major advances in postwar carrier aviation was the introduction of the angled deck, the most significant effect of which was to reduce dramatically the frequency of landing accidents. Amongst the earliest beneficiaries of this new development was 800 Squadron, one of whose pilots is here conducting a 'touch-and-go' in an unmarked Attacker on board the US carrier *Antietam* in the English Channel not far from the Squadron's home base.

FRONT-LINE SQUADRONS

Above: Officers of 800 NAS on the occasion of the Squadron's commissioning in August 1951: (seated, left to right) Lieutenants Duncan Lang and Bruce Clark, Lieutenant-Commander George Baldwin (CO) and Lieutenants Douglas Price (SP) and Ray Rawbone; (standing) Lieutenants Nigel Ovendon, Robin Fluker, 'Lofty' Rouse, Mike Nicholas (AEO) and Don Moore-Searson and Commissioned Pilot 'Bunny' Warren.
Below: On 3 October 1951 the Squadron visited South Marston, the Vickers-Armstrong (Supermarine) facility at which Attackers were manufactured. All eight aircraft flew in, and four are seen here taxying towards their parking slots outside the factory. A photograph of the Squadron taken from the roof of the building visible here is reproduced overleaf.

reason Graeme Rowan-Thomson 'filled in' with individual solo aerobatics. His display was invariably exciting, his low-level, inverted flight had us on the edge of our seats and we were all rather relieved when he had finished!

We carried out mock combats against other fighters—usually RAF Meteors—and in these the Attacker proved to be a very average aircraft. Its gun sight, for example, was only marginally in advance of that fitted to the Seafire. However, we were of course very pleased to receive the

aircraft, and it did provide a valuable service in introducing jet aircraft to the Royal Navy.

800 and 803 continued to fly Attackers until August 1954, when they were replaced by Sea Hawks. Meanwhile 736 Squadron was fulfilling its AFS duties with a mixture of Attackers and Meteors based at Culdrose. I took over this squadron in April 1953 and we moved to Lossiemouth in November that year. When I took command we had about eleven or twelve Attackers but we genuinely struggled to keep them serviceable. Maintenance was of nightmarish proportions, and inevitably a great proportion of the AFS course was carried out in Meteors rather than Attackers. The switch between aircraft types became routine and I cannot recall any problems, although a single-engined land-

Crystals and Snake Climbs *Lieutenant-Commander Don Moore-Searson*

In August 1951 I was reacquainted with the Supermarine Attacker when I joined 800 Squadron, then forming up at RNAS Ford in preparation for embarkation on board the brand new carrier HMS *Eagle*. There were ten pilots in total, and we took turns to fly the eight aircraft that Their Lordships, under the financial constraints of the time, decided should equip the Fleet Air Arm's first jet fighter squadron. This lack of finance also contributed to a measure of parsimonious handling regarding certain aspects of the development of the Attacker, as we in 800 Squadron were shortly to find out. As it happened, for much the same reason, *Eagle* herself was not ready to receive her squadrons until March 1952. Providentially, however, this extra time ashore offered us the opportunity to discover and do something to overcome many of the technical problems that plagued the Attacker prior to embarking in the carrier.

Generally speaking, we found the Attacker to be an enjoyable aircraft to fly. In terms of its performance, it was well able to take care of itself when put up against RAF Meteor 8s flying out of Tangmere, as we proved to ourselves on the many occasions when we were either 'bounced' by them or we ourselves initiated the attacks. The Attacker was also just about able to out-turn the Meteor 8. On the debit side, the aircraft's pressurisation system was only able to sustain a cabin pressure equivalent to 18,000 feet when flying at 40,000 feet, and the cockpit heating arrangement was pretty well useless. When we were operating in the Arctic during Exercise 'Mainbrace', even wearing a combination of four pairs of gloves did little to prevent my fingers

Below: Another photograph of the Squadron's visit to South Marston in October 1951, looking back towards the main runway. Supermarine's 'executive' De Havilland Dominie can be seen in the distance, whilst the statutory airfield emergency vehicles are deployed at far left. As far as can be ascertained, the Squadron, on commissioning, did not apply the tail code 'FD' to any of its aircraft as might have been appropriate.
Right: An 800 Squadron pilot up on an early sortie. The clear cockpit hood was later replaced by a more robust component—as explained on page 50.

ing in a Meteor had to be carried out with care and 'by the book'. The number of Attackers at Lossiemouth was increased to over twenty until they were replaced by Sea Hawks in 1954.

By 1955 all the Attackers had been phased out of the front-line squadrons in favour of Sea Hawks, but the aircraft soldiered on in the hands of the Royal Naval Volunteer Reserve. In the spring, summer and autumn of 1955, respectively, 1831 (part of the Northern Air Division, and based at RNAS Stretton), 1832 (Southern Air Division, RNAS Ford) and 1833 Squadron (Midland Air Division, RAF Honiley) received F. B. Mk 2s. However, these units were all disbanded in the swathe of defence cuts decreed by the 1957 Defence White Paper.

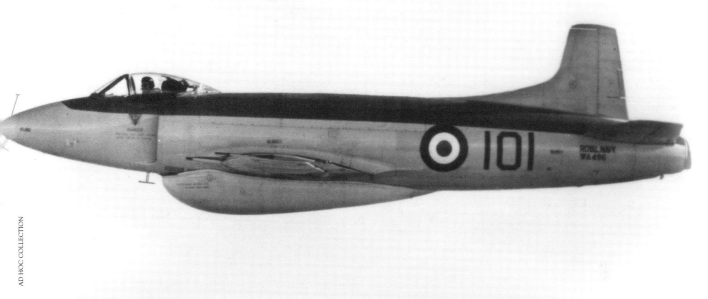

from quickly becoming numb, and when the time came to land back on board it was as if I no longer had any fingers. The pain whilst thawing out was no joke either. Lack of an adequate heating system also caused the inside of the canopy to ice up during a descent from high altitude, making it very difficult to see the other aircraft in the formation.

Whilst we were unable to do anything about the inadequate heating, we did devise a 'quick fix' solution to the internal icing problem by using pieces of four-by-two cloth coated in glycol to wipe over the perspex prior to commencing a descent, our engineer officer arranging for these to be carried in a discarded cigarette tin which he had fitted to the left-hand side of the cockpit.

Two other problems arose from the internal icing. I personally experienced one of them whilst flying from Ford. During one flight, whilst I was drawing fuel from the drop tank, the fuel transfer lever mechanism froze solid and I was unable to move fuel from the internal tanks to the main tank. A rapid descent through 30,000 feet of cloud to the warmer sea level temperature melted the ice and I was able to free the lever. The other internal icing problem we experienced was again whilst flying on the drop tank but this time concerned the freezing of water droplets suspended in the tank fuel. These 'super frozen' droplets collected and combined together in the main fuel filter, where they blocked the flow of fuel. This, again, resulted in the aircraft being left with only the remaining fuel in the main tank, and in this instance the very low fuel temperature in the tank prevented the ice from thawing out until after the aircraft had landed.

It was some time before we were able to discover what had caused the main fuel filters to stop the flow of fuel.

When the problem occurred, it usually resulted in a wheels-up landing on the runway with only the ventral drop tank sustaining minor damage. After jacking up the aircraft and lowering the undercarriage, it was found that the engine would start, having left no evidence about the cause. There were quite a number of these wheels-up landings before the cause was discovered. On this occasion, the fuel filter was opened up where the aircraft had stopped on the runway, and before it had a chance to warm up. Tiny ice crystals were found clinging to the inside. The cure was to put a quantity of methanol into the drop tank together with the fuel to act as an anti-icing agent.

By this time we had all been practising approaches to the airfield from high altitude with a simulated fuel filter failure. The controller would guide us to an overhead position above cloud and then vector us round into a spiral glide, with aim of breaking through the bottom layer of cloud in a position above the airfield from which we could carry out a dead stick landing on the runway. Fortunately we were soon becoming quite good at it when the next problem appeared—again concerning the main fuel filter. This time it was not ice that was blocking it but a sticky mess caused by the fuel acting as a solvent on the material from which the drop tank piping fuel seals had been manufactured. This caused a major hold-up to our programme as we were then about to embark in *Eagle*. We flew aboard with empty drop tanks and immediately began to dismantle and clean them out. All the pilots were involved in helping the ground crews and, on opening up the drop tanks, we found that not only were they covered in sludge but they were also littered with the remains of sundry broken rivets and machining swarf! Supermarine were quick with the excuse that the drop tanks were supplied by a sub-contractor!

In spite of its tail-wheel undercarriage, the Attacker was a nice aircraft to take to the deck. We were, of course, using the American system of deck landing signals that had been introduced in 1949 in order to facilitate cross-operations with US Navy carriers. This system meant we had to carry out circuits at 100 feet instead of at 300 feet as in the British method, and instead of a steady rate of powered approach on to the deck from the end of the downwind leg we now had to maintain height all round the circuit to a position just abaft the round-down, where the 'batsman' gave the 'cut' signal. This, at first, took a bit of getting used to: seeing clear blue water between oneself and the carrier as one closed the throttle was initially a little alarming! From this point the pilot closed the throttle and pushed the stick forward to initiate a quick dive towards the deck. Then he had to ease the stick back to ensure that the aircraft touched down in a three-point attitude and caught a wire without bouncing back up into the air and into the barrier—a skill that was not particularly easy to master. Thus with the jet-powered Attacker, since the engine took a few seconds to wind down when the throttle was closed, the 'cut' was given when the aircraft was still some way astern of the round-down. It is interesting to note that when the British-designed mirror landing sight came along, the US Navy and the Royal Navy both reverted to the original British 300-foot circuit with a steady, powered, descending approach in a three-point attitude right down to the deck.

On 11 March 1953 I had another rather lucky escape. Flying from *Eagle*, which was at that time in the Mediterranean, the Squadron was earmarked to conduct a flypast over the yacht bringing Marshal Tito of Yugoslavia on a state visit to Britain. I discovered that the flight-deck party had spotted my aircraft in the wrong take-off position, and so, as was the convention, I had to climb into the aircraft that had been spotted where mine should have been. All went well until we were due to return to land-on and had extended dive brakes so that we could rapidly burn off excess fuel to get down to landing weight. The aircraft I should have been flying was positioned in the formation just ahead of where I was. Suddenly, smoke billowed out of its jet pipe and then flames appeared at the rear end of the fuselage. I closely followed it down in an increasingly steep dive whilst trying to attract the attention of its pilot. Sadly, I was unable to make contact and it eventually crashed vertically into the sea.

By this time the Attacker had accumulated a considerable amount of time exposed to the salt-laden environment that surrounds a carrier. This opened up a design problem that had not previously been envisaged and it concerned the cockpit glazing structure where, in an attempt to improve the streamlining, a rounded Perspex moulding had been fitted in front of the optically flat armoured front panel and, to equalise the air pressure with that in the cockpit, a tube had been led from the air gap between the two elements of the windscreen to that within the cockpit. However, each time the aircraft climbed and descended, the resultant changing air pressure acted like a pump and introduced more and more salt-laden air into the gap. Owing to evaporation, a layer of salt became deposited within the air gap which, over time as the amount increased, severely restricted forward visibility when landing-on into the glare of the sun. Eventually, in conjunction with another modification to the cockpit hood whereby much of the Perspex top and side structure was replaced by metal, the front streamlined moulding was deleted.

In due course, the development problems both in *Eagle* and with the Attacker were sorted out and the Squadron was able to complete a very enjoyable series of cruises and operate the aircraft to its full capability. Meanwhile the Attacker F. Mk 1 had been developed from being a pure fighter into the fighter-bomber F.B.1 version, and bombing and rocket-firing exercises were routinely carried out. Furthermore, unlike some other jet aircraft as they came into service, there were no early problems with firing the guns as these were originally designed for the Seafang/Spiteful piston aircraft and were located out on each wing, well away from the engine intakes. However, there was a small penalty for this arrangement in that when the ammunition became used up on one wing before the other had finished firing, the subsequent asymmetrical recoil forces caused the aircraft to yaw, which tended to throw the aim off unless it was corrected by the application of some rudder.

It was during this time that the technique called the 'snake climb' was developed. This was to enable a formation of aircraft to be catapulted off in sequence and, without waiting around at low level until the last aircraft was airborne, to climb individually through the layers of cloud until the leader had penetrated to the clear sky above, where all could form up visually. It was achieved by the leader climbing straight ahead until all the aircraft had been catapulted off at five-second intervals, and then calling out any changes of heading. Five seconds after the leader had called the new course, the second aircraft to take off would change to the new course, ten seconds later the third aircraft would change to the new course, and so on, and thus, in sequence, all the formation would be following the leader as he navigated a path to penetrate the layers of cloud. When the last aircraft to become airborne had reached clear sky he would look ahead to locate, visually, the other aircraft in line trailing behind the leader, he would then call that he was 'visual' and the leader would respond by commencing a turn to allow the formation to close up into battle formation.

At the end of an exercise the recovery of a formation through continuous cloud cover to the carrier was achieved by the fighter director sending the formation to the high-altitude waiting position, which would typically be at 20,000 feet or above. With the aircraft now flying in divisions of four aircraft disposed in *en echelon* starboard formation, the Fighter Direction Officer, using the ship's Carrier Controlled Approach (CCA) radar, would call off each aircraft in turn, giving it appropriate descent courses to steer and any necessary altitudes to hold as he guided the formation, one after the other, down through cloud and on to the final course to the flight deck. The turbulent wake astern of the carrier would be seen first and then, when the pilot was able to pick out the yellow jacket and bats of the DLCO, he would announce that he was 'visual', and so on until all the aircraft had been recovered.

There is no doubt that all the development work carried out with the Attacker, and eventually at sea on HMS *Eagle*, facilitated the smooth introduction into service of the later Hawker Sea Hawk, for HMS *Ark Royal* and for the other fleet aircraft carriers. It is, perhaps also important to bear in mind that, from an industrial point of view, the experience gained with the Attacker brought to light many manufacturing, structural and fuel system deficiencies that had been inherited from an earlier time. It also demonstrated that, in spite of ever-present parsimonious Government funding, many problems can be overcome by enthusiastic team work at squadron level.

During my time in 800 Squadron, whilst on occasion there were a number of rather tense experiences with this aircraft, it is interesting to note that in twenty-one months we suffered only one fatality—not too bad a record compared with that of some later jet aircraft entering service.

My last flight in an Attacker was on 15 May 1953 at Ford, after which I went back to QFI'ing at the Operational Flying School on Meteor T.7s and Vampire T.22s with 759 Squadron at RNAS Culdrose, which eventually moved to Lossiemouth. However, on the day I was leaving Ford, and whilst waiting for an aircraft to ferry me to Culdrose, I decided to take a nostalgic stroll through one of the hangars. It was full of brand new Attackers. Somehow I felt drawn towards one in particular. There, in front of me and wearing shiny new paintwork, was WA482, my old NAFDU aircraft, now rebuilt as a Mk 2!

Main image: An Attacker veers away having received a 'wave-off' from *Eagle*'s DLCO (visible at the extreme left). As discussed in this book by the air crew involved, the commissioning of jet aircraft in the Royal Navy led to the development of a brand new type of safety barrier. It is seen here, raised to halt the progress of an errant arrival; two of the old, three-cable barriers can be seen lying flat on the flight deck. Within a few years, the introduction of the angled deck would render all such barriers superfluous.
Overleaf: An Attacker, its tailfin adorned with the 800 Squadron crest, approaches *Eagle*'s starboard catapult preparatory to a launch.

ATTACKER

Stripped Clean *Rear Admiral Ray Rawbone* CB DSC

The world's first jet deck landing was made by Lieutenant-Commander 'Winkle' Brown in a Vampire in December 1945. Plans to equip the Royal Air Force with jet fighters were well under way, and work began in earnest to ensure that the Fleet Air Arm moved forward in unison. Although for the first time ever Royal Navy pilots had a marvellous view of the carrier flight deck during the final approach in a Vampire, the wave-off at low speed caused considerable anxiety because of the slow response from the throttle and poor initial acceleration. The Vampire's Goblin engine was not very powerful—some 2,700 pounds of static thrust—and in consequence the introduction of jet aircraft into front-line Royal Navy squadrons was delayed pending the development of more powerful engines. When the Attacker came along it benefited from having the Nene engine, which offered 5,000 pounds of thrust (and, later, marginally more).

The Attacker was not a demanding aircraft to fly. The tail wheel was a handicap and the aircraft was occasionally difficult to taxi, especially on the flight deck. It was essential to be careful when you turned: you could easily blow somebody away! There were no free take-offs from carrier decks with the Attacker, so all launches were catapult-assisted. There was no propeller slipstream over the tailplane, so keeping straight was perhaps marginally more difficult than with a piston-engined aircraft. The acceleration was pretty rapid, and once you were up at around 100 knots or so you began to get good control. The top limiting speed of the aircraft was about 0.82 Mach, although some pilots claimed to have exceeded this. As you approached this speed, there was a marked nose-down effect which you had to hold back. The rate of climb for a jet was moderately slow, and it took about ten minutes to reach 25,000 feet. The turn was quite good, but although an Attacker could out-turn a Meteor it would probably not have had that advantage over a prospective enemy. The ailerons were nice and light, but the aircraft was very heavy in the looping plane.

The aircraft was quite short-ranged. A 'clean' Attacker might manage 350–400 miles, and if you had the belly tank beneath you that could be stretched to roughly 750. These figures, of course, assume a standard take-off, a climb to, say, 35,000 feet, flying normally without any violent manoeuvres or sharp changes in profile, and landing. If you were actually *fighting* the aircraft, the radius of action—dependent on the altitude at which the combat took place—was only 100 miles or so.

There was a problem with the position of the fuel cocks: the LP cock and the cock controlling fuel from the belly tank were close together, and there were accidents caused by pilots selecting the wrong cock, resulting in no fuel feed. We were prohibited from spinning the Attacker, although, having said that, I can recall in 736 Squadron having a mock dogfight with a student who inadvertently spun his

Below: A hive of activity on board *Eagle* as two Attackers are prepared for take-off. An interesting feature of the new carrier's design was the provision of 4.5-inch dual-purpose (high-angle/low-angle) guns, their turret tops flush with the flight deck so as not to interfere with air group operations. These weapons—there were eight such mountings, one on each quarter—would be progressively removed throughout the ships' career as their usefulness diminished. Those visible here, on the port bow, would be the first to disappear, making way for the angled deck.

Right: An 800 Squadron pilot, his flight-deck handlers surveying the scene from a distance, prepares to start the Nene engine of his Attacker on board HMS *Eagle*; notice the ground starter battery at right. This is the same aircraft as that depicted on page 49, now with the tail letter for *Eagle*. Such code letters generally bore only a coincidental relationship to the names of aircraft carriers at this time and were generally allocated on an alphabetical basis according to the earliest available.

Below: An abrupt halt as an Attacker runs out of arrester cable, suddenly terminating the aircraft's forward progress. A tail-up attitude of his aircraft on arrest was not an unusual experience for an Attacker pilot.

aircraft when he stalled at the top of a high wing-over. He recovered quickly, but generally it was a manœuvre that one did not perform for the fun of it.

The Attacker's cockpit was pressurised, albeit not very effectively; for example, at 40,000 feet the pressure was equivalent to that one would normally experience at about 20,000. The heating system was poor, and prolonged cross-country flights generally resulted in frozen pilots by the time their aircraft had landed. Ejection seats were in the early stages of development and decidedly primitive by today's standards. If a pilot was leaving the aircraft above 20,000 feet, it was wise for him to delay the deployment of the parachute because it could readily be torn. Therefore, once clear of the aircraft, the seat had to be manually detached first. He also had to remember to retract the gyro gun sight before he ejected.

The Attacker's landing speed was higher than that for piston-engined aircraft, although by the late 1940s even these were getting quite fast. The stalling speed for an Attacker with wheels and flaps down was some 90 knots, compared with around 65 knots for a late model Seafire, so the landing approach was made at about 105–115 knots. I believe that the spoilers (as they were originally called) were designed as an aid to short landings, although I cannot recall any of us deploying them in that sense. They were used by the pilots as air brakes.

When the aircraft came into service the carrier circuit changed inasmuch as pilots could now carry out a straight

Left: Not quite as planned: the aftermath of the very first encounter with the new nylon safety barrier installed on board HMS *Eagle*. 800 Squadron CO Lieutenant-Commander George Baldwin's Attacker was certainly stopped in its tracks, but only just—as Rear-Admiral Ray Rawbone explains here. By great good fortune, the 'Boss' was uninjured.

Right: A brush with the barrier by WA487 after heavy landing that missed all the arrester wires during 800 Squadron's first embarkation in March 1952. Flight-deck handlers are rushing to clear the aircraft from the deck: another Attacker is in the circuit (extreme top left of photograph) and receiving a 'wave-off' from the DLCO, whose 'bats' can be seen above the screen. Two of the new safety barriers are rigged—a wise precaution considering the CO's experience!

approach thanks to the excellent view forward. GCA or instrument approaches could also be made 'straight in'. Turning circles were rather wider compared to that of the Seafire (for example), and a little more time had to be allowed owing to the faster approach speed. Once safely on deck, the barrier would go down, you would fold your wings (tips only on the Attacker) and the deck handlers would park you.

These were the days of the axial deck—'bolters' off the angled deck were well into the future—and the barrier was still vital to flying operations. The introduction of the Attacker coincided with the trial and introduction of a new barrier, a rather high and intricate network of nylon which looked like a large line of washing when on a final approach! Our first landings in *Eagle* using this device were preceded by a short briefing by the 'boffins' responsible for its manufacture and trials. We were told that if we were caught up in the barrier the nylon would spread the strain evenly, with no damage to the aircraft, and that, once extricated, the aircraft could be pushed back and the flying programme could carry on as if nothing had happened! The new barrier would save lives—and millions of pounds' worth of repair bills. Needless to say, Flyco was crowded to watch the first landings!

By sheer chance the first pilot to test it was George Baldwin, the Commanding Officer of 800 Squadron. He made a good landing, but as he touched down the bill of his arrester hook broke off and, unretarded, he went straight

Left: Attacker WK322 of 800 Squadron had an encounter with the barrier when coming into land on board HMS *Eagle* in March 1953. Although in this photograph the port undercarriage leg appears not have lowered, it is in fact masked by the vertical nylon 'tapes' of the barrier. The aircraft probably just missed all the wires—and *Eagle* generally had twelve of these rigged (with provision for a total of fourteen).

Right: The aftermath of this incident: the aircraft appears still to be sitting on three legs and has seemingly suffered only superficial damage. One of the old-style barriers is seen on the left, stowed flat across the flight deck; these were still required for stopping propeller-driven aircraft.

into the barrier! None of us had ever seen an aircraft stripped so clean: wings, undercarriage, tailplane—everything was completely ripped off! Indeed, had it not been for the aircraft's sternpost just managing to snag the top wire of the barrier and arrest the aircraft's progress, a manned Supermarine Attacker F. Mk 1 would have slithered, torpedo-like, along the deck and over the bows into the deep! Alarm and embarrassment all round—evident not least on the hitherto confident countenances of the assembled boffins!

We continued to use nylon barriers throughout *Eagle*'s first commission, but no doubt the failure to design a 'damage-proof' barrier added emphasis to the need for the introduction of the angled deck and mirror landing aids: both, together with the steam catapult, were essential to the continued economical use of aircraft a sea.

ATTACKER

New Territory   Captain Keith Leppard CBE

Serving as a flying instructor/batsman at the Operational Flying School (OFS) at RNAS Eglinton in 1950-51, involved in the training of Seafire and Firefly pilots that was to culminate in their first deck landings, was a greatly rewarding experience, and the news that I had been earmarked for jet conversion and appointment as a 'batsman' for the first operational jet fighter squadrons destined for the brand new carrier HMS *Eagle* was therefore received with excitement and delight.

After a short conversion course on a single-seat Vampires at RNAS Culdrose, I joined RNAS Ford, where *Eagle*'s air group was to work up, in summer 1951. Soon Supermarine Attackers started arriving off the production line and 800 Squadron was formed under the command of Lieutenant-Commander George Baldwin, a hugely experienced fighter pilot. 803 Squadron's formation followed, this unit commanded by Lieutenant-Commander Tommy Handley fresh from the Korean War. All the pilots had considerable operational embarked experience except for two sub-lieutenants, Edwin Tomlinson and Ron Davidson, who joined 803 Squadron having been hand-picked from the OFS pipeline. Experience of the first jet fighter operations at sea was to determine whether future OFS graduates could progress straight to operational jet squadrons.

My first flight in an Attacker was relatively uneventful apart from a tortuous taxy between the squadrons' dispersal area and the runway. The small twin-tailwheel configuration which supported a long and heavy jet pipe ensured that alarming swings when taxying were easily induced; flight-deck hangar operations would have benefited had a nose-wheel been incorporated as in contemporary jet fighters, and only the tips of the wing folded, which also compromised deck and hangar space.

The work-up of both squadrons continued apace until the time arrived for training in the ADDLs for which I had been appointed. This was new territory both for myself and for all the Attacker pilots. There were a number of considerations to take into account which differed from those obtaining for piston-engined aircraft. Certainly the most important was the alarmingly slow response to engine-power adjustments, mainly because of the absence of immediate reaction derived from propeller airstream over wing and control surfaces. This was expensively illustrated on one occasion when I was 'batting' an Attacker from the end of Ford's runway and my 'low/slow' signal to the pilot failed to arrest the aircraft's sink into the marshy meadows alongside the River Arun. Fortunately the pilot was unhurt, but there were red faces all round! On the positive side, the view over the aircraft's nose was superb and pilots experienced no difficulty in lining up with the carrier deck.

The air group embarked in *Eagle* in March 1952, heralding a new era for British naval aviation. Apart from the innovation of jet operations at sea, *Eagle* was the largest carrier ever to be commissioned into the Royal Navy. Much of her equipment was untried and new procedures had to be formulated. It was to be a pioneering experience both for the ship and the Attacker squadrons, and lessons were learned day by day. Although the initial land-on of 800 and 803 Squadrons was uneventful, it was not long before a major deck landing disaster was fortuitously averted although an aircraft was written off. Existing carrier crash barriers were considered inadequate for the much higher jet landing speeds, and in their place *Eagle* had installed large, specially designed nylon nets suspended from high metal arms. The theory was that, whereas previously the propeller and undercarriage of aircraft missing the arrester wires were engaged, jet aircraft would be halted by dint of the nylon

nets wrapping themselves around the wings. George Baldwin, returning from leading a sortie, was the first to land back on board. I was 'batting' and at the 'cut' position speed and height appeared to be perfect—as one would expect from a pilot of his experience. To the dismay of all watching, however, the Attacker's arrester hook broke off on touch-down and the aircraft plunged full tilt into the nylon barriers at over 100 knots. Both wings were neatly pulled off with undercarriage legs still attached and enmeshed in the nets. The separated, torpedo-shaped fuselage careered on up the flight deck at considerable speed, but, by an enormous stroke of good fortune, the thin wire suspending the nylon nets from their supporting arms embedded itself in the tailfin. The fuselage was brought to a halt a few feet from the forward end of the flight deck and George stepped straight out, shaken but unhurt. The nylon barriers were considered to be over-tensioned, thus preventing a smoother pull-out. Modifications were hastily embodied and happily there were no further barrier or other jet accidents during my time on board.

In the autumn 1952 *Eagle* took part in the first major naval NATO exercise, 'Mainbrace', in the North Atlantic. The unseasonal foul weather curtailed air operations, but, to the satisfaction of the Attacker squadrons, the US Navy carriers taking part ceased flying some hours before *Eagle* was forced to follow suit.

So ended a fascinating appointment for me, and I returned to the fighter OFS, this time at RNAS Culdrose (and later RNAS Lossiemouth). My rôle was as before the *Eagle* experience, but this time training 'pipeline' *ab initio* pilots on Attackers for their first deck landings and subsequent service in embarked squadrons. The splendid performance of the two 'sprog' pilots, Tommy and Dave, in the *Eagle*/Attacker experiment demonstrated that inexperience was not a bar to front-line jet appointments, and this was a big step forward.

The jet nylon barriers were short-lived, and after trials (involving George Baldwin and other Attacker pilots) on board the USS *Antietam* the angled deck concept was proven and adopted in carriers worldwide; barriers were no longer required, neither for jets nor for any other type of aircraft. This British invention, together with the mirror landing sight and the steam catapult, revolutionised all aircraft carrier operations and was a great tribute to Royal Navy designers, engineers and aircrew. In my view, the first commission of HMS *Eagle* and her Attackers contributed in no small measure to these impressive advances in the history of the Fleet Air Arm.

Below: New technology: an Attacker lands on board HMS *Eagle* in 1952. The 'batsman'—more correctly the Deck Landing Control Officer, or DLCO—is visible standing in front of his screen at far right.

They Can Also Bite
Commander Graeme Rowan-Thomson

Every so often in one's flying career the unexpected happens: a bit of equipment stops working, or the weather suddenly turns foul on you, and, whilst your adrenalin output may hit the roof, you hope that your training and experience will see you through and will result in a happy outcome. Occasionally, no amount of training or experience can help.

So it was on 11 March 1953, when I was serving in 800 Squadron. We were embarked in HMS *Eagle* in the Mediterranean. We had a full air group of two Attacker squadrons, one Sea Hornet and one Firefly squadron and a flight of Skyraiders, and we had spent the last month exercising in the Med, so we were well worked-up in the technical sense. Thus, when the signal came through from 'on high' that we were to mount a mass ceremonial flypast in honour of Marshal Tito of Yugoslavia, the general feeling was that we could take this in our stride. Apparently he was paying an official visit to Britain, part of which included time on board one of Her Majesty's ship in the Mediterranean, and no one had any qualms about mass flypasts.

The briefing was straightforward. As I recall, the Attacker squadrons would lead, with 24 aircraft in six flights of four, in 'vic' formation (that is, as in the fingers of one's left hand. As a lowly junior pilot I was flying in No. 2 (little finger) position, formating on the leader of the flight on my right, with the other two aircraft the other side of him; flights were 'stepped down' so that the leader of each flight was looking slightly upwards to the one ahead. The front man of all was at about 1,000 feet; I can't remember the speed. I had my eyes fixed on my leader and we were all in a tight, precise formation as we flew over Tito. It seemed to have gone very well.

It was at that point that I suddenly saw flames coming out of the air-pressure balancing flaps on either side of the engine of the aircraft being flown by my flight leader: there was no warning black smoke, no explosion—just evil, angry red flames devouring his Attacker. The metal fuselage melted, in seconds it seemed, showing the skeleton of the frame for a brief moment before it, too, was enveloped in fire and smoke and the aircraft started its terminal dive into the sea. The radio was full of calls, jamming each other but all telling the pilot to bail out. There was no way in which he could survive this inferno and control the aircraft: there was no hope and he had to get out of it fast. But he wouldn't, or couldn't, and he was lost with his aircraft.

I don't know what the findings were of the subsequent Board of Inquiry; it was perhaps a massive fuel leak from a burst pipeline, or maybe from a split tank, and I don't know why the pilot failed to eject. I did not see him even try to get rid of his hood, as the prelude to ejection, so it could be that there was some mechanical damage or personal injury which prevented it, for the pilot was a skilled aviator with many hundreds of hours flying to his credit. However, no amount of training or experience could overcome this kind of disaster.

The day did not end there, for two Sea Hornets collided after the flypast, with the loss of three aircrew, and, much later during the visit, I believe the Royal Air Force gave a display at which they also lost a pilot. Marshal Tito subsequently asked that there be no further flypasts in his honour!

Below: *Eagle*'s air group at around the time of the disastrous events described here by the author. Four of 809 Squadron's Sea Hornets are seen in the foreground.

Above: With the mandatory planeguard destroyer on station, an 890 Squadron Attacker crosses Eagle's round-down. This photograph was taken on 3 April 1954 during Exercise 'Medflexable' (sic), involving ships of various Allied navies; it was during this cruise that the incident described here by the author occurred. The Pilot's Notes advised that, for deck landings, 'The recommended final approach speed at maximum deck landing weight (full ammunition and approximately 125 gallons of fuel remaining) is 105 knots. . . . Engine r.p.m of between (sic) 9,700–10,000 will be required on the approach to maintain a constant height with undercarriage and flaps down. At a lower landing weight the final approach speed may be reduced by 2–3 knots but a speed below 105 knots leaves very little in hand for obeying the batsman's signals.'

Below: 800 Squadron's Attacker WZ284 is towed towards Eagle's deck park during 'Medflexable', steered with the aid of a trolley at the tailwheel.

FRONT-LINE SQUADRONS

HMS *Eagle*'s company mans ship for the carrier's arrival at Gibraltar during her Mediterranean cruise in the spring of 1954; the Spanish port of Algeciras is out of frame to the left. Within a few weeks 800 Squadron—whose aircraft are here ranged on the flight deck and carry side numbers from all three allocated series—would disband at Ford; 803 Squadron, which by the time this photograph was taken had disembarked its aircraft to Hal Far, finally relinquished its Attackers a little later, in August 1954, and the type passed from front-line service. Its successor was the Sea Hawk, four of which, assigned to 806 Squadron, bring up the rear of the two columns of jets seen here. A pair of anti-submarine Avengers and, behind them, two AEW Skyraiders, complete the visible inventory.

Coming-To at Ten Thousand Feet *Commander Tommy Handley*

The first operational Attacker squadron, 800 NAS, was formed at RNAS Ford in mid August 1951 under the command of the famous World War II aviator George Baldwin, and the second squadron, 803, formed with eight aircraft in November 1951 under my command, also at RNAS Ford. My Senior Pilot was W. D. D. ('Mac') MacDonald and several other quite famous pilots—Dick Reynolds, Des Russell and Bill Black—were also appointed.

The Attacker was the first operational jet fighter to see service with the Royal Navy, and the only British jet fighter to have a tailwheel as opposed to a tricycle undercarriage. It was said that the Navy wanted to get jet aircraft on carriers at sea in the early 1950s, and, as the RAF was getting priority, the only possible candidate was the Attacker (which was, in truth, the flying test-bed for the Rolls-Royce Nene engine).

The Attacker was a reasonably easy aircraft to deck-land. The main advantage over previous aircraft was that the pilot had an unobstructed view of the ship when coming in to land, although as we were using the USN deck-landing technique it was necessary for him to 'round out' before coming on board with his aircraft: it was not until we changed our technique in order to utilise the mirror sight (and were flying Sea Hawks with tricycle undercarriages) that we were able to fly our aircraft in a steady descent of about three degrees 'to the deck', that is, all the way to touch-down. One had to be wary of the relatively slow reaction of the early jet engine to any sudden increase in throttle movement that might be required for acceleration in order to prevent a stall. This was brought home to me on one occasion whilst on finals prior to landing on HMS *Eagle*. I was a little slow and the batsman gave me the signal to increase power—and then promptly dived through his escape hatch and disappeared! I increased power and speed, and then cut the engine, rounded out and caught the

803 NAVAL AIR SQUADRON

Located at RNAS Ford and (briefly in spring/summer 1954) RNAS Hal Far, and on board HMS *Eagle*

Commission
26/11/51–04/11/54 (Attacker F.1s 26/11/51–00/01/53, F.B.2s 00/12/52–0010/54)

Commanding Officers
Lt-Cdr T. D. Handley, Lt-Cdr J. M. Glaser (12/01/53), Lt-Cdr W. D. D. MacDonald (19/05/53), Lt-Cdr J. S. Bailey OBE DSC (04/06/53), Lt-Cdr T. G. Innes AFC (02/06/54)

Senior Pilot(s) (known)
Lt-Cdr W. D. D. MacDonald

fourth wire. On another occasion, having landed and picked up a wire, the end of the hook snapped off and I was left careering up the deck at high speed. The barriers were lowered in error (!), but I managed to bring the aircraft to a halt with the use of the brakes. Quite exciting!

Internal fuel tanks in the Attacker held only 290 gallons and at max revs at low altitude one could use all of that in twenty minutes whereas a normal sortie was of forty minutes' duration. Hence most of the time, and always when operating from the carrier, we carried the external

FRONT-LINE SQUADRONS

Right and below: Lieutenant-Commander Tommy Handley, CO 803 Squadron, brings Attackers WA527/'103' (right) and WA519—the Squadron flagship, call-sign '111'—into land on board HMS *Eagle* in 1952. The flaps are at maximum droop and for both landings the cockpit canopy is open. WA519 carries the Squadron crest beneath the windscreen quarterlights on the port side.

Main image: The 803 Squadron CO catches the wire in WA519 for another successful shipboard landing. The Deck Landing Control Officer keeping a watchful eye on things in this image taken on board HMS *Eagle* in 1952 is none other than Lieutenant (now Captain) Keith Leppard, another of the contributors to this book.

belly tank containing 250 gallons of kerosene. The tank was rather large and unwieldy and reduced the fine flying characteristics of the aircraft; it also reduced the top speed low down by some 40 knots. These tanks cost the Navy £850 each—the same as a new Ford Zephyr 6 in 1951!—and we were told that they were only to be jettisoned in the event of a dire emergency. On one occasion one of our aircraft had a complete engine flame-out at high altitude.

The pilot made an excellent forced landing, wheels-up on the belly tank, at Ford. There was no damage to the aircraft, merely to the external tank. The undercarriage was lowered and the aircraft was towed round to dispersal. The engineers removed the tank and then tried to start the engine. It fired up quite normally at the first attempt, and indeed the aircraft could have been flown immediately. The problem was found to have been caused by a very small amount of water in the kerosene. The fuel can hold small amounts in suspension quite readily and this does not affect the operation of the jet engine, but at high altitudes and at very low temperatures the traces in the fuel from the external tank froze in the fuel filter and this prevented fuel reaching the engine. Of course, with the aircraft on the ground, after a period of time the ice thawed and the engine worked as advertised.

One day I took off with my No. 2, W. G. 'Blackie' Black, for an exercise flight. By the time I had reached 25,000 feet

I was almost unconscious and flying erratically—although I did not realise it. My No. 2 immediately understood what was happening and flew ahead of me, rolling and turning to attract my attention. I managed to follow him down to about 10,000 feet and at this stage I came-to, feeling hot, sticky and confused. I broke away and landed, realising that I had been suffering from a lack of oxygen. The oxygen had been turned on 'high' the whole time since start-up and was indicated to be flowing quite normally. However, immediately prior to my flight the aircraft had been on inspection, which had required the removal of the ejection seat, and on the seat being replaced the mechanic had connected the radio cable but not the oxygen tube. As a result of this incident it became standard practice before start-up for aircrew not only to check that the oxygen was on and indicated to be flowing but to puff into the mask as well.

During 1952, 803 Squadron came to fame in the aviation world by starting up a formation aerobatic team. Four of the pilots had done this sort of thing before in piston-engined aircraft and were keen to continue to hone their skills. Rocket rails and bomb carriers had not at the time been delivered to the squadrons, so our operational flying training was restricted, and this gave us time to take on and train for this additional enterprise. The four concerned were Bill MacDonald

(Leader), Dickie Reynolds, Des Russell and Bill Black, who developed a first-rate performance centred on a box formation. Indeed, they became quite special, and word soon got around. They put on a display over the Britannia Royal Naval College at Dartmouth, at various Air Days (including that at Exeter), at RNAS Lee-on-Solent for the Flag Officer (Air) Home and at the prestigious King's Cup Air Race at Newcastle. They were invited to perform at an International Air Day in Holland, but after a good deal of practice (and anticipation) for this event our Attackers were grounded on account of the fuel problem mentioned above. The Powers That Be decided that it was vitally important to resolve the issue quickly and get the aircraft back into operational front-line service as soon as possible. They were right of course, but it was disappointing for our display team.

I must say that being involved with the introduction of jet aircraft to the carrier was exciting, if a trifle hair-raising at times. It was the future: we were flying brand new aircraft as opposed to the twenty-year-old types we have in service today. Without a belly tank the Attacker was a very pleasant aircraft to fly. It was not designed for high speed and would probably make only Mach 0.7 in level flight, 'clean' with no external racks, weapons or drop tanks. In a shallow dive and at full throttle it could make Mach 0.78, at which point the nose started to go down and nothing would stop it: the only way to return to normal flying was to close to close the throttle and put the air brakes out. Radios and our only navigation aid, the YE beacon, worked reasonably well, but the more we electrified our equipment the fewer the number of serviceable aircraft we had on the line at the end of the day.

The Attacker served its purpose, but we were pleased to see it replaced by the Sea Hawk—which was designed for the deck and was in almost every respect a thoroughbred.

Like their station-mates 800 Squadron, early in their commission 803 Squadron paid a courtesy visit to the Supermarine facility at South Marston and put on an air show, and once again the company photographer was on hand to take a series of superb images: this is one of them. The side numbers have all but one been cunningly (!) concealed by upturned wing tips and impedimenta, but the Squadron crest can be discerned on the tailfin of the Attacker in the right foreground. Lieutenant Bill MacDonald is occupying the cockpit of the aircraft nearest the camera; an Attacker destined for the Pakistani Air Force is visible in the background; and the pre-delivery FAA aircraft in the far distance at left has yet to receive its full paintwork.

Main image: Preparing for departure: 803 Squadron Attacker pilots await the order on board HMS *Eagle*. Each aircraft has its catapult strop looped around the forward IFF antenna beneath the nose, ready for attachment to the shuttle, and the flight deck crews stand by, ready to assist each launch.
Right: 803 Squadron officers in informal pose at a rain-soaked Ford early in 1952: (left to right) Nigel Ducker, Bill MacDonald (SP), 'Dave' Davidson, Ron Shilcock, Tommy Handley (CO), Dick Reynolds, 'Tom' Tomlinson, Des Russell, Nick Bailey and George ('Bill') Black.

FRONT-LINE SQUADRONS

Does It Tumble When Ditched? *Captain A. W. ('Hap') Chandler USN*

My introduction to the Supermarine Attacker took a somewhat circuitous route, which began when I was informed of my selection as an exchange pilot to join the Royal Navy's first operational jet squadron. I had just returned from a Mediterranean cruise as Operations Officer of VF-21, a squadron flying the Grumman F9F-2 Panther, one of the US Navy's earliest jets, aboard the USS *Franklin D. Roosevelt*, one of our large straight-deck carriers.

When my wife, baby girl and I arrived in England in August 1951, I reported to 781 Squadron at Lee-on-Solent. This was to teach me 'the British way' in which flight operations were conducted. I was checked out in the piston-engined Fairey Firefly with dual touch-and-go's (or 'circuits and bumps', as the British say) and a short solo syllabus comprising beacon homing, QGHs, cross-country and forced-landing practice. Not only was I reverting to dealing with the propeller 'p' factor, this bird's propeller turned the other way ('anticlockwise') and I had to get used to using *left* rudder when applying power instead of applying right rudder. Coping with the standard British hand brake, instead of the toe brakes I had used throughout my entire flying experience, generated some interesting moments!

The Attacker squadron had not yet been formed, so I was then sent to RNAS Culdrose to join 702 Squadron, commanded by Lieutenant-Commander Peter Perrett. The squadron flew De Havilland Vampire and Gloster Meteor jets. I no longer had to deal with a propeller—but I was still left trying to master that hand brake! 702 Squadron transitioned pilots to jet airplanes, familiarized other designated officers with jet operations and, as a matter of fact, trained some pilots destined to man the first jet squadrons.

One of the highlights of my tour at Culdrose was meeting Lieutenant Lygo, who had been an exchange pilot with the US Navy flying the twin-jet McDonnell F2H Banshee fighter. Ray gained a reputation as one hot pilot by, among other feats, actually shutting down an engine to practice single-engine landings in the Banshee; it was our Navy's standard operating procedure just to bring one throttle back to idle to simulate the loss of an engine. At that time, Ray, CO of 759 Squadron, the Fighter Weapons School at

Below: An 803 Squadron Attacker on the point of launch from *Eagle*'s starboard catapult as another aircraft departs from the port. The retractable cupolas ('howdahs') between the tracks housed the senior ratings whose job it was to fire the catapults on the direction of the Flight Deck Officer. The FDO would circle his green flag above his head to tell the pilot to come up to full power and the pilot would respond with a 'thumbs-up', signifying that all was well and that he was ready. The FDO would look to Flying Control to confirm that it was showing a green 'traffic light', and he would then glance ahead and drop his flag. That was the signal to the rating in the cupola to fire the catapult.

Culdrose, was kind enough to personally check me out in the Seafire 17 (the Navy's version of the legendary Spitfire) and the twin-engined Sea Hornet. I am eternally grateful to Ray for those memories, which I will always treasure.

Even though I was enjoying 702 Squadron, I was getting discouraged as my tour was ticking away and I was still not in the promised first jet squadron. Ray again came to my rescue one night during a dining-in, during which he successfully fortified me with a couple of pink gins followed by some Horse's Necks and finally convinced me to approach the senior officer present, Admiral Sir Rhoderick McGrigor, with my problem. Trembling in my boots, I spoke to the Admiral—and, lo and behold, the very next day I had a signal to report to 803 Squadron at RNAS Ford within the week! I must admit that before I received the signal I reviewed in my head how I had ruined my career, how I would be sent home in disgrace, how I would be forced to resign and, worst of all, how I should have to tell my wife what I had done. (I didn't have the courage!)

I enthusiastically checked into 803 Squadron and promptly met the very impressive Commanding Officer, Commander Tommy Handley, along with his skilled pilots and highly professional crew. The Squadron went right to work putting me through their ground school syllabus in preparation for my first flight. I recall my concern about being able to track straight down the runway while gaining the speed required to raise the tail and, once airborne, how much effectiveness would I have with the manual flight controls instead of the boosted control surfaces of the F9F-2. I was also concerned about the soft helmet (as opposed to the US Navy's 'hard hat' I had been used to) and the 'demand' type oxygen mask vented to the atmosphere (unlike the pressure oxygen mask I was used to). I was thankful that I had become familiar with this equipment while with 702 Squadron, although I was not totally convinced that it was giving me all that I required! However, I eventually realized I could find no difference other than comfort between the two.

The day of my first flight arrived—22 January 1952! The Attacker's response to takeoff throttle was a little quicker than the Panther's and the tail rose rapidly, which allowed precise tracking down the runway. The Attacker had levers where the F9F used switches, but this was of no consequence to me. The stick forces were well harmonized, but a bit higher in the Attacker compared to the F9F, and the roll rate of the F9F was faster because the Panther's controls were hydraulically boosted. The grouping of the flight instruments, if not exactly like the Panther's, was close enough that flying in instrument weather was a smooth transition.

Deploying with 803 Squadron aboard HMS Eagle on their first cruise since the Squadron was formed was very exciting for me. In shipboard operations, the Attacker was a delight: it was agile on the deck, had excellent visibility over the nose, and was solid and allowed precise stick and throttle control during the carrier approach and landing. For a new airplane, the Attacker provided a surprising low

Below: Officers of 803 Squadron at RNAS Ford, photographed in the summer of 1952: (seated, left to right) Des Russell, Bill MacDonald (SP), Tommy Handley (CO), Dick Reynolds and Don Titford (AEO); standing) Nick Bailey, 'Hap' Chandler, Nigel Ducker, Bill Black, 'Tom' Tomlinson and Ron Davidson.

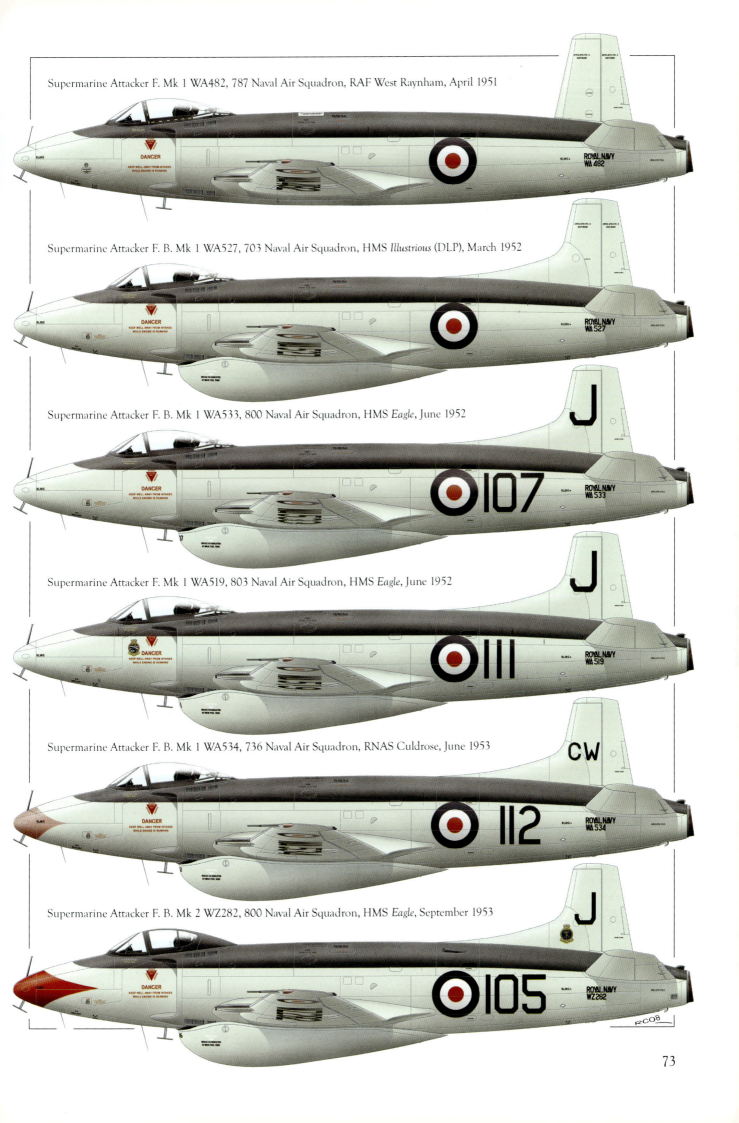

FLOWN BY THE AUTHOR

SUPERMARINE ATTACKER F. Mk I
WA492, 890 Squadron,
RNAS Ford, July 1952

ATTACKER

Supermarine Attacker F. Mk 1 WA487, 767 Naval Air Squadron, RNAS Stretton, September 1953

Supermarine Attacker F. B. Mk 2 WZ280, 736 Naval Air Squadron, RNAS Lossiemouth, February 1954

Supermarine Attacker F. B. Mk 2 WZ299, 718 Naval Air Squadron, RAF Honiley, September 1955

Supermarine Attacker F. B. Mk 2 WZ283, 1831 Naval Air Squadron, RNAS Stretton, January 1956

Supermarine Attacker F. B. Mk 2 WZ288, 1832 Naval Air Squadron, RNAS Ford, April 1956

Supermarine Attacker F. B. Mk 2 WZ292, 1833 Naval Air Squadron, RAF Honiley, October 1956

maintenance per flight hour, giving us excellent availability. We completed the summer cruise accident-free—almost.

At the completion of the cruise I discovered that I was one of the lucky ones to have been assigned to fly one of the Attackers back to Ford. I had already loaded my airplane with what it could carry, including a silver cup generously given to my daughter by the Captain and officers of HMS *Eagle* on the occasion of her being christened in the Ship's Chapel. We launched aircraft on 8 July 1952 before the *Eagle* entered Portsmouth Harbor. I was preflighting my aircraft when our Engineering Officer advised me that my plane had just been signed off by Maintenance, and we went over some of the various items that had been worked on. After I was settled in the cockpit, engine start was normal and all systems checked out okay. I taxied forward to the self-aligning rollers and was hooked up to the starboard catapult. I advanced the throttle to takeoff power, all indications looked good, I put my head against the head rest and I signaled to the Catapult Officer that I was ready to go.

Early on in the launching stroke I heard, and felt, a low-order explosion. By the end of the stroke, and as I began flying, I realized the jet was not responding correctly to my control inputs. Even though the engines were reading normally, I continued to experience low-order engine explosions. I kept thinking, 'Am I in trouble or not'? Was I ever—'Wings' radioed and told me I was on fire. I tried to climb to the minimum safe ejection altitude, at that time 2,500 feet, while monitoring the fire to see whether it would go out, but I quickly realized that was not going to be an option—the plane just wasn't gaining altitude. I began smelling smoke, and at that point two things flashed into my mind: I'd better shut down the engine before it blew up, and I recalled that there was a belief that the Attacker would tumble end over end if it were ditched. At that point I had no other options.

Fortunately, having just launched, I was aligned straight into the wind. I closed the high-pressure fuel cock to shut off the fuel flow to the engine and the Attacker became a glider. I was pleased that the Attacker didn't drop like a rock but continued gliding, which allowed me—or so I thought—to pick out the piece of swell I wanted to land on. I recall that my first contact with the water was quite a bit more gentle than I was prepared for, thanks to the Attacker's inherent flying qualities and the good fortune of there being a mild sea state. The second and third final impact, however, was much more violent and I had to hang on for dear life. I attribute my survival to the workmanship and rugged construction of the Attacker, and that the Attacker inherently was not subject to tumble end over end.

When the plane came to a stop everything worked as advertised. I activated the harness quick release, freed the dye marker, and performed all the other post-ditching items we practiced—except that I must have stayed in the cockpit a little too long congratulating myself while doing a body inventory. When I finally climbed out of the cockpit standing on the gunwale, and was reaching in grabbing the

Below: Lieutenant 'Hap' Chandler poses with his Attacker—the complete naval fighter pilot although not quite the complete fighter aircraft since, for the moment, it lacks its cannon armament. The photograph was taken during the Squadron's visit to South Marston shortly after it was commissioned—see also pages 62–63.

dinghy, the airplane started sinking! Not only was it sinking, it was pulling me with it as the dinghy was lodged under the instrument panel! I finally got the picture, let go of the dinghy, and popped to the surface.

Once on the surface, I saw the ventral (belly) tank floating several feet away from me, smoking, as if to tell me about the important part it had performed in absorbing the impact and possibly even preventing the Attacker from tumbling. The rest of the plane was on its way to the bottom of the Channel—unfortunately with my daughter's christening cup.

I was taken aback by the extreme quiet as I floated by myself in the middle of the English Channel. Shortly, however, I heard the noise of a whaleboat being lowered from HMS *Ulysses* and the stroke of the coxswain setting the rowing tempo for the ship's Boys' Division.

Now that I realized I had survived the ordeal, there was time for a little humor as the members of the Boys' Division hauled me in over the gunwale onto the forward thwart (first seat of the boat). I obviously hadn't done a complete job of tearing the dye marker pocket out from the life vest to fully release it. The marker, a blue/green/yellow glob the size and shape of a bar of soap, fell out on the seat and I muttered, to no one in particular, 'Did that come out of me?' The boy with the bow hook fainted. I then took a serious second look to make sure it really *wasn't* part of me!

To the best of my knowledge, I believe I am the only person ever to have ditched an Attacker. This being the case, I'm glad that the possibility of it tumbling upon ditching turned out not to be true!

The men of the Royal Navy with whom I served were real aviators and mariners, having all the attributes of true gentlemen. I am very proud of and treasure my service in the Royal Navy and I would consider it an honor to serve with them again. I thank them for the memories of a lifetime.

An epilog. The Captain and Officers of HMS *Eagle* graciously replaced my daughter's cup, which, to this day, is one of her favorite and most treasured possessions.

Below: WZ290, a late-production Attacker on the Squadron, is catapulted from HMS *Eagle* towards the end of the Squadron's commission. This photograph illustrates the dangers of jumping to conclusions regarding the Squadron identity of an Attacker by relying merely on a call-sign that may be visible. Officially, 803 Squadron numbered their aircraft in the '110' series, but in practice although 800, 803 and 890 NAS were allocated numbers in the '100', '110' and '140' series, respectively, for the purposes of exercises and deployments the aircraft on station were in effect 'pooled' and pilots flew whatever happened to be available. Thus, for example, an Attacker with a side number in the '100' series and carrying the swords and trident could be temporarily assigned to 803 Squadron (i.e., the 'wrong' unit), and even, while so allocated, be flown by an 890 Squadron pilot.

Above: The officers of 803 Squadron photographed at Ford in December 1952, by which time the Squadron establishment had increased from eight to twelve aircraft and five additional pilots had joined the unit: (seated, left to right) George Black, Des Russell, Bill MacDonald (SP), Tommy Handley (CO), Dick Reynolds, Donald Titford (AEO) and Nigel Ducker; (standing) Johnny Rawlins, Derek Monsell, Tommy Young, Nick Bailey, Max Morris (USN), Peter McDermott, Mike Howland, Ron Davidson and 'Tom' Tomlinson.

Above: An 803 Squadron Attacker seen at Ford in late 1953; Fireflies and Harvards are visible in the far distance. Again, the call-sign is 'wrong' (and, unusually, is geometrically slightly awry). Pilot Peter McDermott has his name carried on the nose of the aircraft—though of course it may not be he who is sitting on the cockpit.

Below, centre (left to right): Three from a sequence of some dozen frames taken on board HMS *Eagle* on 26 January 1953 and showing the fate of 803 Squadron's Attacker WP276 (Lieutenant Bill MacDonald, Senior Pilot). The arrester hook failed on contact with the wire but, fortunately, the braking was such that contact with the barrier was relatively docile. The third image depicts 'all hands on deck' in the best Naval tradition as a veritable army of personnel lifts the heavy barrier free from the aircraft.

Bottom (left, to right): Another sequence showing a barrier entrance, this one depicting rather more velocity and its consequent effect on the airframe. The accident, on *Eagle* on 23 June 1953, occurred after the pilot of WP304, Lieutenant A. F. Brown, unfortunately missed all the wires, and it can be seen that the upper athwartships cable of the barrier, echoing 800 Squadron CO George Baldwin's experience, sliced into the tailfin to bring the aircraft to a halt. In this case only one wing was ripped away. As in the previous sequence, the Attacker is an F.B.2 and has the later type of cockpit canopy.

Above and below: 800 and 803 NAS aircraft on *Eagle*'s flight deck in early 1953 during the Mediterranean Cruise. In the photograph above, both types of cockpit hood are evident, and one aircraft lacks a belly tank. In terms of markings there is little homogeneity: although theoretically there are two Attacker units here, both establishments had recently taken on former 890 Squadron aircraft (and, for that matter, former 890 Squadron pilots). In fact, for practical purposes—throughout their existence—the front-line Attacker units operated not so much as individual squadrons as an integrated Wing. Bottom: Snapshots of Attacker men, taken during the Cruise: (left) J. M. Glazer (CO 803 Squadron) and Dick Reynolds; (right) Bill MacDonald (SP 803 Squadron, left), Dick Reynolds, Des Russell and Peter McDermott in front of *Eagle*'s 'batting' screen.

Above: 803 Squadron's officers about May 1953, back at Ford following disembarkation: (seated, left to right) Nigel Ducker, Bill MacDonald (SP), Bill Bailey (CO), Dickie Reynolds and Bill Black; (standing) Peter McDermott, Johnny Rawlins, Dickie Jenkins, Mike Howland, Tommy Young, (unidentified) and Tommy Tomlinson.

Below: At Ford following the autumn 1953 cruise: (foreground, left to right) (unidentified), Eddie Ward, Dickie Reynolds, Mike Howland and Dickie Jenkins. Peter McDermott is in the cockpit and Tommy Young is leaning over it. The new-fangled 'bone dome' worn by Eddie Ward is evidently not yet standard issue!

ATTACKER

Above: All-weather operations—1: part of the snow-cleared flight-line at Ford, winter 1953/54.
Right: All-weather operations—2: *Eagle* turns into the wind in order to launch an Attacker, autumn 1953; others, alongside the island, are preparing to depart. Sea Hornet night fighters, Firefly anti-submarine aircraft, Skyraider 'early-warners' and an Avenger are ranged aft, awaiting their turn to fly.

Above: A searchlight on the island blinks as a red-nosed Attacker lands on board *Eagle*, February/March 1954.

Below: 803 Squadron's officers on board *Eagle*, spring 1954: (seated, left to right) Peter McDermott, Bill Bailey (CO), Tom Innes (SP) and (unidentified); (standing) Colin Casperd, Mike Howland, Tommy Young, Don Dorling, Dickie Jenkins and Eddie Ward. The mascot is Caroline Lockhart, the daughter of Lady Penelope Lockhart and sister of Sub-Lieutenant Lockhart RNVR, the permanently absent (because fictitious) member of 803 Squadron and the star of outrageous in-squadron pranks.

Opposite, upper: HMS *Eagle* approaches Mers-el-Kébir in French-held Algeria for a courtesy call, spring 1954. Even by this time, old-style cockpit hoods were still evident on some Attackers. The ship's Dragonfly helicopter is ranged forward. This visit was not without intensity: it was here, some fourteen years earlier, that British battleships had wrecked a significant part of the French Fleet, with the loss of over 1,000 lives, to prevent its falling into German hands. Anglo-French relations were severely strained for some considerable time afterwards.

Opposite, lower: Two photographs depicting the wreck of WP300, which, following a power failure, crashed at Hal Far on 2 April 1954. The pilot, Lieutenant J. S. Binney, survived unhurt.

You Can't Take It with Water
Commander Graeme Rowan-Thomson

After 890 Squadron formed in April 1952, we spent a happy summer familiarising ourselves with this new aircraft—propelled by blow rather than fan-power—and welding ourselves into an operational squadron, with activities ranging from the flamboyant (formation aerobatics) to the serious (live weapon-firing) and always improving our instrument flying skills so that we could fly in bad weather with the same confidence as in clear skies. There were a multitude of exercises, formations and drills to learn, particularly for the 'sprog' pilots, all aimed at getting us properly worked-up to a state where we could embark in a carrier and complete the task at sea, our true environment.

As with the two other Attacker squadrons, 800 and 803, our carrier was to be *Eagle*, the largest RN ship to be launched since the end of the war and suitably modified to operate jets, which meant that the barriers were of nylon construction and so designed that the impact of the aircraft going into them would be taken by the wings rather than, as with piston-engined aircraft, the nose. This was a quite necessary modification when one considers that the nose of a jet contains the pilot whereas a piston aircraft has a propeller, an engine and a few other bits of aeroplane at the front to absorb the shock and protect the occupant of the cockpit.

Towards the end of the summer, an embarkation date was fixed . . . and, for reasons unknown, promptly altered. Summer slid into autumn and winter, and it was not until 27 October that we got airborne to embark. The plan was that we would fly north to Milltown, a satellite airfield to

Above: The author prepares to come on board HMS *Illustrious* during deck-landing practice, 16–17 July 1952. The apparent anachronism of a jet aircraft with a tail-wheeled undercarriage has often been remarked upon; the comment not so frequently made is that, as the Attacker effectively had the wings of a piston-engined Spiteful/Seafang, the arrangement could hardly have been otherwise.
Left: Two further photographs—a sequence— taken during 890 Squadron's DLP. This aircraft is WA482, and the tail-up attitude as the wire is drawn was not untypical.
Right: Early arrivals for 890 Squadron at Ford, June 1952. WA524 was very quickly thereafter transferred to 736 Squadron and never received a side number during its brief sojourn in Sussex. In the lower photograph, the pilot has boarded and the electrical connections have been made; once the ground crewman has fixed the retractable cockpit entry step, the Nene will be powered up and taxying will commence.

Lossiemouth on the Moray Firth, and embark in *Eagle* some time on the 29th. The ship herself was also working up, so we had to slot in with her programme.

When we manned aircraft at Ford in the morning of the 27th, it was a pretty filthy day. There was a solid base of cloud which looked as if it went on up a long way, and the Met. were not forecasting anything much better at Milltown. The Squadron started up and all eight aircraft checked in on the R/T, and then I discovered that I had a hydraulic leak somewhere in my port wing. Consternation— and a quick change of plan was called for. The Squadron would fly off as planned, leaving me to follow on once the leak was fixed, and with an experienced pilot to lead me.

So it was, some two or three hours later, that I took off for Milltown on the wing of my section leader. The Met. had not been wrong. We went into cloud at about 1,000 feet and remained in it all the way up to 30,000—and then stayed in it! The entire flight took about an hour and a half, of which nearly an hour was on instruments. This was not a great struggle for a practised pilot, and we were all up to it, but to formate on another aircraft in cloud for that length of time *was* a strain. I could not look at my instruments at all, I had no visual references outside the cockpit beyond my leader, and both of us were cocooned in fog. Writing of this some fifty-five years later, I still remember suffering the most appalling attack of vertigo I've ever had. I was

890 NAVAL AIR SQUADRON

Located at RNAS Ford and on board HMS *Eagle*

Commission
24/04/52–03/12/52 (Attacker F.1s 22/04/52–00/00/10/52, F.B.1s 00/07/52–00/10/52, F.B.2s 00/07/52–00/12/52)

Commanding Officer
Lt-Cdr R. W. Kearsley

Senior Pilot
Lt R. D. Taylor

convinced that we were in a steep turn, a spiral dive, climbing and probably at the top of a loop, and it required a supreme effort to ignore these signals from my natural balancing systems and concentrate on staying close to my leader. Had I been able to read my own instruments and not bother about formation flying, the vertigo would have

ATTACKER

Opposite: Images of the RNAS Ford Air Day on 6 September 1952. In the photograph centre left, the author is shown at 400 knots and fifteen feet AGL along the main runway. It is an unusual photograph: he was normally inverted while carrying out this demonstration! The general view shows that, as well as the Station's Attackers, an impressive array of Sea Hornets and Meteor trainers was on display.

Main image: Attackers prepare to depart from Culdrose in decidedly inclement weather for the Battle of Britain Flypast, 15 September 1952. Sea Hornet night-fighters and Sea Furies are lined up in the background. Attacker '143' is nominally an 890 Squadron aircraft.

Above: Life at Ford, 1952: Dennis Whitton (left) and 'Tinker' Taylor. Petty Officer Osborne his men inspect WK325's Nene.
Left: The culprit: a sample of the contaminated fuel that caused all the problems (see pages 49 and 65).
Below. The joyrider. Unbeknownst to air crew and gound crew alike, 890 Squadron's WK328 took a rodent aloft one day, scurrying around in, of all places, the engine casing. It emerged alive following touch-down at the end of an hour-long flight, although presumably sweating and with a serious headache. At left, the evidence is held aloft, having been put out of its misery; at right, an inspection is carried out of the stowaway's temporary living quarters. Very few of 890's Attackers bore the Squadron crest, although this one clearly did.

Above: The Fleet Air Arm fighter pilot, 1952: the author, ready for flying, while serving with 890 Squadron.
Below: WA493 departs from HMS *Eagle*, the catapult strop irrecoverably falling away into the sea. During embarkation on *Eagle* in March 1952, this aircraft was officially allocated to 800 Squadron, but within a couple of weeks it had 'swapped' units and was being utilised, with no change in its markings, by 890 Squadron. The steam streamer indicates the direction of the wind-over-deck.

gone in seconds or been very considerably reduced: that is the benefit of constant instrument flying practice. Luckily, it disappeared, as it does, after two or three minutes.

When we arrived at Milltown we got a standard let-down through cloud, but the base was high enough to permit a normal visual circuit and landing—and a wonderful sight met our eyes. At first glance it looked as though 890 Squadron had decided to park all over the airfield more or less at the end of their landing run, but the reality was less dramatic. Of the six aircraft that had gone ahead of us, four had made it to the Squadron dispersal site, one was well into the runway overshoot and some yards off the centre-line, while the sixth aircraft was lying on its belly in the long grass at right angles to the duty runway! It appeared that both the latter had suffered engine failure at height but within gliding range of Milltown. Both pilots had made a very good job of coming down through 30,000 feet of cloud with a dead engine to land within the airfield perimeter.

The cause of the engine failures in both cases was fuel starvation, and the cause of the starvation was water in the fuel in such quantity that it froze up in the engine filters and blocked them solid. As we were all fuelled from the same source at Ford before we left, perhaps the rest of us were lucky! Certainly there were red faces at Ford, but we never discovered whether the water contamination was in the main fuel storage tanks, which would have affected a range of aircraft, or possibly only in the bowser that took the fuel from the tanks to 890 Squadron.

Whatever the answer, the Squadron AEO drained all the aircraft and filled them up with pure, unadulterated, Scottish fuel before we flew again, for our next trip would be to embark in *Eagle* at sea, where there were no large, flat airfields for emergency landings.

Later in the year, the pilots attended a meeting with Rolls-Royce at Derby to discuss, amongst other things, this propensity for the freezing-up of the fuel as there was beginning to be a history of the problem; Lieutenant Kettle, for example, had had a freeze-up at Ford in 890 Squadron. I'm afraid I never did find out what was decided as I left the Squadron soon after that!

FRONT-LINE SQUADRONS

Above: Two photographs showing the post-landing inspection of WA484 following an accident at Ford in September/October 1952, the circumstances surrounding which are not known. It would appear that a belly tank was not fitted to the aircraft for this particular flight.

Stand to Attention! *Lieutenant-Commander Tommy Young*

Early on in 890 Squadron's commission I and three colleagues were forming up in a finger-four north-west of Arundel. Suddenly someone called that it looked as though I had a hydraulic leak. He came close underneath me and recommended that I put the undercarriage down and return to base. As I turned for home and put my wheels down, there was a louder than usual *thump* and paraffin vapour started to issue from the cockpit demisting and pressurisation pipes, depositing itself across the windscreen. These quickly turn to small blue flames, at which point I made for the sea.

I was at about 2,000 feet. The aileron controls then started to burn through and I found myself spiralling towards the ground. I immediately raised my left hand and pulled the blind. A metal tape had jammed part of the ejection seat mechanism, with the result that the second charge did not fire and, when I was free from the aircraft, the seat was tumbling around with me still connected to it. I managed to kick the seat away and went into freefall, cartwheeling as I descended. I remembered the Medical Officer telling us to stand to attention if ever this happened! I then found myself going down head first (which I actually found to be an extremely pleasant experience).

The ground was now coming up very fast, and so I pulled the ripcord. The seat came shooting past me, travelling very quickly. I landed in Binstead Park, and the keeper's wife, living nearby, found me. After brushing myself down, I thumbed a lift along the main road and without further ado made my way back to Ford, a couple of miles away. I rang the Control Tower, who, having heard nothing as to my whereabouts, were quite exercised about the incident. My response—that I was sitting in the Ward Room—took them somewhat by surprise. The Senior Pilot, 'Tinker' Taylor, wanted to know the details the next morning, but the incident was taken in its stride; we all took the attitude that these sorts of happenings were not much more serious than falling off a horse.

FRONT-LINE SQUADRONS

Above left: Lieutenant Tommy Young, 890 Squadron, Ford, 1952.
Above right: The smoking crater caused by WA493's impact with the ground, 13 May 1952.
Lieutenant Young was only the second FAA pilot in squadron service to have been obliged to use an ejection seat—which was at the time very much a new 'toy' and regarded with a good deal of awe.
Below: Lieutenant Mike Howland at 35,000 feet over Salisbury Plain during a Squadron exercise.

Rolling and Gliding
Lieutenant-Commander Tommy Young

The Scimitar was my favourite aircraft, and the Sea Fury was also a delight. The Sea Hawk was viceless. The Attacker, however, was something of a mishmash. It had an enormous ballast weight in the nose, some three inches thick from memory, mainly because the wings were stuck on too far forward! It also had something of a reputation for catching fire—something I can appreciate from personal experience.

Our CO in 890 Squadron, Bobby Kearsley, was quite a character although possessed of a short fuse on occasions. One of his favourite tricks was, when leading a finger-four, to take his aircraft down to the deck and then start to execute a starboard turn. Those aircraft *en echelon* starboard, of course, had nowhere to go, and the poor chap on the inside (usually 'Mac' McDermott) was forced to break away from the formation. The debrief afterwards was, shall we say, passionate. The final time he led the aerobatic team—at Lossie, I believe—the cloud base was not very helpful. He came in across the airfield, and instead of barrel-rolling (which of course you have to with a formation), he carried out an individual roll, scooping it out at the end very close to the ground. The rest of the team had to haul on their control columns for their lives. He then formed up, brought his team in from the seaward side, pulled up to do a loop, disappeared into the cloud and just continued climbing almost into a stall. Another trick was near-missing the lighthouse! 'Tinker' Taylor, the SP, led the aerobatic team after that.

On one occasion during Bobby Kearsley's tenure as CO 890 Squadron, I spent the best part of one detail getting as high as I could and then rolled over on full throttle, pointing at the ground. The Mach number built up pretty quickly, but when I closed the throttle it immediately felt as though someone was whacking the aircraft with a sledgehammer. One of the trials pilots had experienced something similar, I briefly recalled at the time, and he had had to bail out. I therefore had to open the throttle again (still pointing at the ground!), and the elevators, which did not have power-assistance, seemed to be locked fast. The warming air at lower levels caused the Mach number to drop rapidly, and the aircraft pulled out. One good thing about the Attacker was that, the faster you went, the better the nose-down trim (that is, you trimmed up). Thus, when you slowed the aircraft, its natural tendency was to lift its nose; pulling out of a dive was somewhat eased because of this. The Meteor had the opposite tendency, and this must in some part surely explain the extraordinarily high loss rate amongst the 'young lions' of the RAF. Even with both hands on the stick, it was often too late. (It got to the stage that we were remarking on the 'daily Meteor'.) The Attacker had 'spoilers', intended to assist in deck landing, but I do not recall our ever landing with them deployed. We did try to use them as air brakes, but they were pretty hopeless for this task as well.

The cause of the early fires was eventually found: what at first appeared to be a hydraulic leak turned out to be a fracture in the HP fuel line going through the plenum chamber. We later began flying on Avtur, which gave a better performance but posed a different problem. The Admiralty decreed that, on board ship, the fuel should be displaced with salt water (as for other types of fuel). Unfortunately, this caused emulsification, and most of our aircraft were affected in this way, blocking up the transfer valves from time to time. The Attacker had an 85-gallon

Below: A mishap brought about when WK329, a brand new Attacker recently delivered to 890 Squadron, got too low and too slow on approach during ADDLs at Ford in August 1952 and stalled on to the far bank of a road that ran at right angles to the runway and about 100 yards from it. The aircraft bounced over the road and hit the undershoot, but ended up on the runway. It was an impressive approach, and the pilot, Lieutenant Morris USN, was fortunately not hurt, although a lady driving along the road as the Attacker bounced over her almost had terminal hysterics before she could continue her journey! As can be seen in the third photograph, the belly tank cushioned the impact, although, in the event, not sufficiently to permit the aircraft ever to fly again.

Above: An Attacker at altitude, *sans* belly tank, eases into the photographer's viewfinder. This aircraft was briefly assigned to 890 Squadron (call-sign '141') during April 1942 and was flown by the author from RNAS Ford on a number of occasions.

tank which fed directly to the engine, and fuel from all the other tanks was routed through it. The tank never floated at its full capacity—65 gallons or thereabouts was the normal level. On occasion, it would start to float at lower levels, which generally presaged trouble—for example, when we were flying up to Milltown from Ford, with the objective of joining *Eagle*. The cloud was eight-eighths up to about 30,000 feet, and north of Edinburgh, as my colleague Graeme Rowan-Thomson has mentioned, Peter Ree and Mick McDermott hit trouble. One landed wheels-down and the other wheels-up, gliding into Lossie from somewhere not much further north than Perth! The Attacker glided quite well, if rapidly; the sink rate was about three miles per 1,000 feet.

Later in the commission, while embarked on *Eagle*, we were carrying out a cross-country exercise somewhere over Sicily, my main fuel tank was slipping from 50 down to 45, and to 40, and I decided to call up the ship explaining that I was not sure whether I would make it back. There was complete panic on board (being something of a rebel, I rather relished all this!), and, in the event, they let me come straight in. I picked up a wire, taxied and shut off the engine, and it was discovered that I was down to about five gallons—a few minutes' fuel.

TRAINING SQUADRONS

Note: Duties, locations and names of officers in the table below are those pertaining when Attackers were on establishment.

702 NAVAL AIR SQUADRON
Naval Jet Training and Evaluation Unit, based at RNAS Culdrose.

Commission: 04/04/49–26/08/52 (Attacker 1s 00/03/52–26/08/52)
Commanding Officers: Lt (A) A. B. B. Clark, Lt-Cdr N. Perrett (03/05/51)
Senior Pilot(s): Lt L. A. Jeyes

718 NAVAL AIR SQUADRON   *Believed no crest sanctioned*
RNVR Jet Conversion Squadron, based at RNAS Stretton and RAF Honiley

Commission: 25/04/55–31/12/55 (Attacker 2s throughout)
Commanding Officer: Lt-Cdr W. G. Cook
Senior Pilot(s):

736 NAVAL AIR SQUADRON
Advanced Jet Flying School (Operational Flying School Part II), based at RNAS Culdrose and Lossiemouth

Commission: 26/08/52–26/03/65 (Attacker 1s 26/08/52–00/08/54, 2s 00/00/53–00/08/54)
Commanding Officers: Lt-Cdr N. Perrett, Lt-Cdr P. H. London DSC (01/12/52), Lt-Cdr A. R. Rawbone AFC (20/04/53)
Senior Pilots: Lt-Cdr L. A. Jeyes, Lt A. J. Tallin (00/04/53–00/10/53), Lt-Cdr P. Curry (00/10/53–00/11/54)

767 NAVAL AIR SQUADRON
Component of Naval Air Fighter School, based at RNAS St Merryn

Commission: 01/05/50–08/05/70 (Attacker 1s 00/02/53–00/03/54, 2s 00/07/53–00/03/54)
Commanding Officers: Lt-Cdr D. O'D. Newbery, Lt-Cdr L. J. Baker (09/11/53)
Senior Pilot(s):

COURTESY GEOFF WAKEHAM

Opposite page and right, upper: Although it did not receive Attackers until the spring of 1952, 702 Squadron had since 1949 been the Naval Jet Evaluation and Training Unit, introducing Fleet Air Arm pilots to the techniques required to fly Meteors and Vampires. Soon after the unit had taken delivery of the new aircraft, an accident befell Lieutenant Al Fyfe in WA475: on 4 June 1952 his Nene engine failed, and although he attempted a glide landing at Culdrose his Attacker crashed and was severely damaged. The pilot, happily, survived. It is difficult to determine whether the aircraft has a representation of the Squadron crest on the port side of the tailfin or whether some twisted metal gives the impression of such.

Right, lower: 718 Squadron re-formed in the spring of 1955 for the exclusive purpose of retraining RNVR pilots to enable them to fly jet aircraft, and photographs of their mounts are not abundant. This is WZ302, an F.B.2, carrying the rather dramatic (and quite unofficial) diamond-framed flaming torch insignia adopted by the unit.

Below: Officers of 736 Squadron *circa* September 1952 after its formation out of 702 NAS (with which unit many had been serving): (seated, left to right) Joe Tallin, Len Jeyes (SP), Pete Perrett (CO), the Squadron AEO (name not recalled) and Keith Leppard; (standing) Lieutenant Mee (?), Peter Cort, Al Fyfe, Harry Bain, 'Boot' Nethersole, Lou Tagliarde and (unidentified).

ATTACKER

Mouths Open *Commander J. H. ('Boot') Nethersole*

The Jet Conversion Squadron at Culdrose, No 702, was equipped with Meteor 7s and Sea Vampire 5s until, starting in mid-1952, Attackers began to replace the Vampires and we could start to train pilots to fully qualified standards so that they could replace aircrew in 800, 803 and 890 Squadrons. In due course 736 Squadron completed its rôle as the Operational Flying School Part II (Sea Fury) and 702 took over its tasks, changing its number to 736 in the process.

It used to be said that the only reason Supermarine designed the Attacker was to get some jet experience, using the Spiteful's wings and undercarriage. The Royal Air Force did not want it, having committed to the Meteor and the Vampire, but for the Royal Navy it was an opportunity to get some jet experience at sea more quickly than they would have done had they waited for the Sea Hawk.

The aircraft was generally pleasant to fly 'clean' and, thus configured, had a performance comparable to that of the Meteor, but its internal tankage was limited, so much so that, in order to achieve a reasonable sortie length, we always flew with the large belly tank fitted. However, this tank was not metered, so we would take off on internal fuel, switch to the external tank when airborne, and change back to internals when the 73-gallon collector tank gauge started to go down, the transfer from internals then topping up collector tank which actually fed the engine. This system proved to be my downfall, leading to the only flying accident of my career!

Pete Perrett had led an instructor sortie on a pairs stream take-off from Runway 30 at Culdrose and snake climb for battle drill above the cloud. I was in WA511, flying with Joe Tallin in the fourth section and concentrating on him during the entry into cloud at about 1,000 feet until breaking clear at 30,000. A fuel gauge check showed me that the collector tank was less than half full, and selecting internals did not improve the reading. Now on button 'A', I called that I was downwind for an emergency landing on 30. On finals, I was a little distracted to see a Sea Fury stream take-off in progress on Runway 24 and so, momentarily, did not realise that everything had gone very quiet.

I could not stretch the glide to reach the airfield in the air, so, having just cleared the workshop area hangars, I sank gracefully on to a small patch of grass but with the concrete-posted, barbed-wire fence looming. Differential braking enabled me to point the cockpit between two concrete posts and on course to pass through a gap between the goofing cars on the public road. Happily, the port wing came off at the first fence and I arrived on the airfield in an undignified heap without hitting the goofers or their cars.

The next problem was the hood: it would not wind open, nor would it jettison—something urgently required as the aircraft was now on fire. I undid the parachute and harnesses and stood on the dinghy pack in an effort to heave the lid off with my back. No go—I'd forgotten to undo the dinghy clips and so could not straighten my legs! That snag corrected, however, the hood fell away at the third heave. During my speedy exit another tank caught fire with a *whoosh*, causing flash burns to my face between oxygen mask and helmet.

Goofers were by now causing problems as they had followed the aircraft through the gap in the boundary fence and were standing in a semi-circle around me with their mouths open, There was no visible reaction when I implored them to preserve themselves from the danger of more tanks going up. Luckily, at this point the Captain appeared round the peritrack in his car: he, Captain Rolfe, took one look at me and ordered me to take his car and disappear to the Sick Bay while he took steps to disperse the onlookers.

Later, I listened to the control tower tapes, and these confirmed that other transmissions had jammed all of

Above and below: Two photographs showing the aftermath of Lieutenant 'Boot' Nethersole's unconventional arrival at RNAS Culdrose in Attacker F.B.1 WA511 on 19 August 1952.

mine. Thus Control did not know that I was had crashed on the Runway 30 threshold; indeed, they were unaware that I had been returning to the airfield. Hence no emergency services had been alerted until I was safely tucked away in the Sick Bay!

The next day, 'Little F', Willie Simpson, rang me to tell me to meet a friend of his, who was holidaying in Cornwall, at the main gate as his son wanted to see some aircraft. We looked at 809's Sea Hornets and 759's Seafires, Vampires and Firebrands, and then, approaching 702, I remarked that he would not want to see the Attackers, those 'dreadful aeroplanes'. 'Oh yes I do,' retorted the boy. 'My dad designed them!'

Swiftly I escorted Mr Smith into the Senior Rates' crew room, where the assembled aviators proceeded to bombard him with their criticisms of the aircraft, its serviceability and its maintenance problems. He was very good, making notes of all he was told, which he said would be very useful when designing the next aeroplane. Bless me—it was the Scimitar!

A few months later I went on leave and my mother instantly noticed the last brown remnants of the burn scars on my face, demanding to know the cause.

'Oh, my girlfriend sloshed me with her handbag!'

My mother believed me—and I was somewhat put out!

A Dicey Roll *Commander Giles Binney OBE*

I first met the Attacker in September 1953 down at Culdrose on the Front Line Jet Conversion Course (FLJC) to which I had been catapulted (so to speak) from Lossie and which I remember approaching with some trepidation. I hadn't realised quite how far away Culdrose was, and so, with my Morris Minor heavily loaded *en famille*, the journey down, which I had decided to do in one day, lasted well into the night. Yet somehow in those pre-motorway and low-density-traffic days, one seemed to travel faster.

The course started with conversion to the Meteor—and this I found quite a shock, especially the asymmetric stuff at low speed/high power—and progressed to the Attacker. I particularly remember that, after three weeks or so at Culdrose and about ten Attacker hours, for the first (and, incidentally, the last) time in my flying life I became aware of actively disliking an aeroplane and seriously considering whether I wanted to go on. .

However, in time this passed, and with the help of a splendid group of instructors, including old friends such as 'Boot' Nethersole and Keith Leppard, and the CO, Ray Rawbone, I started to enjoy it. Even so, the aircraft never became a real friend, in the way that, for example, the Sea Fury had done. I seem to recall one particularly alarming characteristic, whereby, with a set of red emergency lights placed around the cockpit coaming, as one turned with the sun abaft the beam they would all, in succession, light up. There were stories of pilots ejecting in a 'knee-jerk' reaction as a result—apocryphal, perhaps, but nevertheless readily believable.

After two months and some fifty hours in the Attacker I found myself returning to Lossie suddenly transformed into an instructor with 736, with our CO again Ray Rawbone and with many of the Culdrose crew. By this time I had even begun to like the aircraft, although I never felt that I had it subjugated. Was I, or was it, in charge? A major attraction, of course, was that on a single-seater jet one was sitting right up front and could actually see where one was going—a benefit especially welcome when, with *Illustrious* cruising in the Moray Firth, Ray arranged for the Squadron to get access to her deck. Suddenly it all seemed so easy. We were very lucky in our CO, who was adept at steering people such as myself into understanding the different principles involved in flying jet and piston-engined aircraft.

After a while, with summer and the Lossiemouth Air Day approaching, we were carrying out an acceptable formation aerobatics display, which on the day went down well. Towards the end of the set piece, 'Boot' and I were briefed to approach, head-on, fast and low, from opposite ends of the main runway, carrying out a co-ordinated slow roll in the process. As I zoomed across the airfield, upside down and not at all sure that everything was working out, there was a shout of 'Christ!' on the R/T. It was Boot's

Above: 736 Squadron officers at Lossiemouth during the first half of 1954: (seated, left to right) Keith Leppard, Pete Curry (SP), Ray Rawbone (CO), Pat Grant (AEO) and 'Boot' Nethersole; (standing) Ted Pepper, Giles Binney, Toby Davis, Jim Rutherford, T. P. Henry (Assistant AEO) and K. S. Brown (ALO).

Below: Mk 1 WA486—see also pages 33 and 35—whilst on duty with 736 Squadron and wearing the old Culdrose (i.e. 'Cornwall') tail code; the latter was changed to 'CU' in 1953. It will be noticed that the paint demarcation line along the after fuselage is still in the original style.

voice. How, I wondered could he have seen my dicey roll? He was of course referring to *his* dicey roll! We were later told that between us we had brought the crowd to their feet.

By now 736's time with the Attacker was drawing to a close. After only six months, and from my point of view a total of only 160 hours and twelve deck-landings, the beautiful Sea Hawk appeared and the halcyon days began.

Left: 736 Squadron students were afforded the opportunity to carry out Deck Landing Practice and for the most part this was problem-free, but an exception was a particularly tragic occurrence on 20 January 1953, when Commissioned Pilot Barker, in WA492, was landing on board HMS *Eagle*. The hook failed during the arrest and the Attacker veered off to port and over the side. The pilot lost his life.
Below: Happier times: the Squadron in an immaculate line-up at Lossiemouth, spring 1954. Two of the aircraft still have the Culdrose tail code; two others have none. The six aircraft nearest K17 hangar, incidentally, do not have white tails: whether by design or by accident, all have their rudders angled to port, catching the sun!
Right, top: The Squadron in formation with their Lossiemouth quarters in the background.
Right, centre: En route from Culdrose to Ford the year before, for the Coronation Review.
Right, bottom: Another 736 Squadron DLP incident, though here with less catastrophic consequences: WA533 appears to have suffered a collapsed port undercarriage leg. HMS *Illustrious*, 1954.

TRAINING SQUADRONS

Slightly Hazardous Captain Jack Worth

My acquaintance with the Vickers Supermarine Attacker was short-lived as my 82 hours on type were in Operation Flying School II in 736 Squadron at Lossiemouth, and the aircraft was taken out of service soon thereafter. Despite its rather bizarre make-up and related idiosyncratic behaviour, I do have fond memories of the aircraft. Why? Because I was an inexperienced student excited to fly anything, especially since it was to be my first single-seat aircraft, therefore no instructor aboard.

As I recall, the Attacker was built as a test-bed for Vickers' first venture into the jet fighter era. It seems incredible (with hindsight) that the RN decided to procure it because it was a hybrid, a mish-mash with an unbelievable tail-wheel configuration and Spiteful wings tacked on, with a totally inadequate fuel capacity of about 375 gallons. Moreover, unlike any jet before or since, the stick had to be pushed forward for take-off in order to raise the tail. Fortunately, it was built around the reliable R-R Nene engine.

Recollections remind me that tail-wheel taxying was not the easiest compared with subsequent jets, with the wheel unlocked, and; a poor air-pad braking system did not inspire confidence over long distances. I once gave 802 Squadron a fright when taxying back from the other side of the airfield. The brakes failed and the aircraft aimed itself straight at their offices and hangar. The aircraft stopped in time—but only just.

Left: WA488, not at Culdrose (as might be suspected) but at Lossiemouth—in a photograph probably taken within a few minutes of that seen on page 86 (and with the rudder turned slightly to port!). 736 Squadron's Attackers, often aircraft 'inherited' from front-line squadrons, displayed a quite remarkable variety of styles in terms of their call-signs—presumably inherited also was a wide variety of stencils with which the maintainers in the paint shop worked!—and some aircraft retained the red nose flash with which they arrived on establishment.
Opposite, top: The Squadron en masse at Culdrose in mid-1953, prior to the transfer to Lossiemouth. Theofficers seated are (left to right) (Assistant AEO), (unidentified), Dave Crofts, Peter Cort, Peter Curry, Joe Tallin (SP), Ray Rawbone (CO), Pat Grant (AEO), Keith Leppard, Al Fyfe, 'Boot' Nethersole and (ALO).

From Lossie to Hal Far Lieutenant-Commander Brian Giffin

I first flew the Attacker in November 1954 during OFS II at RNAS Lossiemouth. The very first problem was squeezing into the cockpit—with the 'cheek' intakes the width available was very limited, as indeed was the fore-and-aft dimension. In this case a maximum thigh length (to assure safe ejection) was imposed, and I believe several tall aviators were excluded. The second problem was taxying: the Attacker was the only tail-wheeled jet to serve with British air arms, and a huge amount of power was required to get the aircraft moving. Bearing in mind also the wide-track main undercarriage, applying the brakes could get you facing the wrong direction in a very short time as a result. Nobody on my course actually managed to get to the end of the runway for his first solo before zig-zagging off the peritrack and getting bogged! I recall that, once airborne, the Attacker was a pleasant aircraft to fly, if somewhat heavy—none of us of course had the experience of powered controls—and that it was particularly suited to ground-attack operations because of its inherent stability.

As the course progressed, our minds were more and more concentrated on our first deck landing, and in preparation we started ADDLs at the satellite airfield at Milltown. Before doing so, we stood with Keith Leppard at the batsman's position at the end of the runway, where he briefed us regarding the finer points. The circuit was flown at 200 feet, and I remember watching a Lieutenant Dunbar (Fleet Entry) from the downwind position. Keith had explained that he would briefly disappear from view behind a line of tall conifers and would start to give signals from the 90-degree position. The only snag was that he did not reappear! The pilot executed an unforced landing without too much damage to the aircraft or to himself. As can be imagined, this did nothing for our confidence! Initial deck landings were carried out on HMS *Indomitable* in the Moray Firth, and thanks to the empty straight deck and no barriers these were concluded without incident.

On completion of OFS II we were sent out to Malta to join 803 Squadron, based initially at Hal Far. The reliability

About a third of the trailing edge of the wing was used for flaps for landing, resulting in a marked aerodynamic effect on selection. Despite heavily stressed briefings to push the stick firmly forward, the first 'downwind' usually resulted in the aircraft climbing like a lift when the flaps were selected. On first solo, most students ended up going around again in order to get back to circuit height.

Once airborne, the Attacker flew quite well and proved a reasonable platform for weaponry, both air-to-air and air-to-ground. On the debit side, however, several other factors came into play. The pressurisation system was barely adequate, the cockpit heating was virtually useless, and when the aircraft was descending from high altitude the interior of the canopy iced up badly.

The air brakes were pop-ups out of the wing roots, which gave extremely poor retardation, while with throttle, air brake and flap levers all together in the throttle quadrant, inadvertent selection of flap instead of air brake lever resulted in some hilarious (if slightly hazardous) incidents in such manoeuvres as formation practice and tail chases.

The maximum Mach number in the Attacker was 0.8 or thereabouts, beyond which the controls locked solid. In tail-chases at medium level, the No. 4 in a loop rarely stayed in touch with the rest of the flight because he usually reached 0.8 Mach and the aircraft just carried on down until the thicker air at lower levels came into play—another cause for amusement at the debriefings.

The fuel system, too, demanded close monitoring. Because of the aircraft's inadequate capacity, a 250-gallon belly tank was fitted, but this fuel was not available until a certain amount had been used out of the main tank and a control selection made for transfer. However, beyond a further certain level, if the belly tank control had not been actuated this fuel could not be transferred. Obviously, if forgotten, this could lead to some embarrassing situations.

In retrospect, nevertheless, despite all the Attacker's foibles, as a student I enjoyed the experience and even managed to win the Fighter School Trophy. There is no doubt also that after the Attacker I found all subsequent jet aircraft to be much easier to convert to and fly.

Right: Attacker WK320 following a wheels-up landing at Lossiemouth on 23 February 1954. The photograph perpetuates the truth, remarked upon elsewhere in this book, that, certainly as far as Attacker markings are concerned, appearances can be deceptive: despite its 'J-for-*Eagle*' tail code letter and the hornet of 803 Squadron adorning the unit crest, this aircraft was at the time employed by OFS II and, therefore, assigned to 736 Squadron. Unusually, too, the call-sign on the underbelly tank does not match that on the fuselage.

of the Nene engine was not high, and several accidents resulted from its failure. Very sadly, my twin brother was killed when his engine failed at the point of take-off. We had been through training together, and although we were very well aware of the dangers associated with naval flying (having already lost two members of our course), this was yet another reminder of the risks we all took.

I stayed with 803 Squadron and in August 1954 we re-equipped with Sea Hawks. In total, I flew the Attacker for just over 180 hours and made nineteen deck landings. My memory of the aircraft will always, of course, be coloured by the experience of losing my brother, but nevertheless, if I can take a dispassionate view, I will remember it as a unique machine—once you got it off the ground!

RNVR SQUADRONS

Note: Duties, locations and names of officers in the table below are those pertaining when Attackers were on establishment.

1831 NAVAL AIR SQUADRON

Part of Northern Air Division, based at RNAS Stretton.

Commission: 01/06/47–10/03/57 (Attacker 2s 00/05/55–10/03/57)
Commanding Officers: Lt-Cdr (A) F. Morrell RNVR, Lt-Cdr (A) H. V. Rougier RNVR (23/04/55)
Senior Pilot(s):

1832 NAVAL AIR SQUADRON

Part of Southern Air Division, based at RAF Benson

Commission: 01/07/47–10/03/57 (Attacker 2s 00/08/55–00/11/56)
Commanding Officers: Lt-Cdr M. R. H. Shippey RNVR, Lt-Cdr (A) T. C. Fletcher RNVR (30/09/55), Lt-Cdr (A) A. J. Austin RNVR (12/07/56)
Senior Pilot(s):

1833 NAVAL AIR SQUADRON

Part of Midland Air Division, based at RAF Honiley

Commission: 15/08/47–10/03/57 (Attacker 2s 00/10/55–10/03/57)
Commanding Officers: Lt-Cdr (A) D. G. Jenkins DFC RNVR
Senior Pilot(s):

Below: WZ294 and a companion aircraft displaying the winged greyhound insignia of 1831 Squadron.

Right, top: Personnel of 1831 Squadron in 1956: (seated, left to right) Bill Brennen, Jimmy Widdop, Peter Rougier (CO), Pete Barlow, Ron Williams; (standing) Mick McClay, Geoff Holden, Ian McDade, Doug Croll; (insets, far left) Don Ranscombe and Don Baines; (inset, far right) Duncan Shaw.

Right, centre: WZ283 of 1831 Squadron with an 'adornment' atop the winged greyhound insignia in the shape of a 'bone dome'— signifying that this aircraft is the CO's customary mount.

Right, bottom: The same aircraft, showing the official Squadron crest displayed on the tailfin and the somewhat stylised nature of the tail-code letters.

ATTACKER

Pride Before the Fall *Lieutenant Bob Neill RNVR*

I managed to achieve many of my flying ambitions during National Service: being selected as a pilot in the Royal Navy at RAF Hornchurch, passing the Admiralty Interview Board—I cannot now remember which came first, but I do remember the shock on my Housemaster's face when I asked for time off to attend these events! No one, but no one, joined the Navy: everyone was expected to go to the Mons Officer Training Unit and join The King's Shropshire Light Infantry, the unit that 'sponsored' the school CCF. The award of my Wings at Syerston by Admiral Caspar John was a proud moment for both me and my parents. (Father said that the Navy drill was not what he expected!) They enjoyed the presentation to me of the Aerobatic Trophy, and I thought that my flying ability was better than the 'Average' rating on the RAF Form 414A stuck in my log book.

Seafire 17s at Yeovilton were the highlight of my experience, and indeed these aircraft were one of the reasons I joined the Navy in the first place, since I knew that the RAF would have phased out its last Spitfires before February 1954, by which time I could have hoped to have got my Wings. I had grown up during World War II and the magic of the Spitfire was very real. I was awarded a tankard for being the best student on the course.

After Yeovilton and Operational Flying School Part I, my colleagues and I joined our RVNR Air Divisions, which for me meant HMS *Gamecock*, at Bramcote, where 1833 Squadron had Sea Furies and 1844 had Fireflies. More pride came when we did our carrier qualification on HMS *Illustrious* in October 1954 and I was called up to Flyco to meet Commander (Air) and to receive a 'Well done, my boy!' from him after my tenth arrival. I was just twenty years old at the time.

We loved our Sea Furies and we flew with no restrictions about how much we did, but 1833 converted to jets during annual training in 1955, when 718 Squadron arrived to undertake this duty in Vampire T.22s. My first Attacker flight took place on 20 August 1955, and the aircraft came to us with an uncertain reputation. We loved the improved performance but we disliked the way it handled compared to the Fury (which was a real 'pilot's aeroplane'). It had very poor high-altitude performance and a low Mach threshold. We christened the aircraft the 'Claptacker'.

There were a number of accidents and incidents involving the eight aircraft that had been allocated to the Squadron. I had a canopy shatter at 39,000 feet but as the aircraft flew satisfactorily at slow speed I elected to land back at base. Some of my Squadron suggested I should have ejected, because if we lost some more Attackers we might get Sea Hawks sooner! R/P firing and 20mm cannon attacks on a towed banner made for interesting flights, as it was during these that you knew how good, or not, you really were. We carried out a large number of sorties on our duty days.

1833 Squadron, the fighter component of the RNVR's Midland Air Division, was due to go to the deck during the two weeks' annual training later that year. HMS *Bulwark* was the carrier earmarked to receive us, but because of the Suez Crisis this never happened. On the day in question, 15 July, I was detailed to carry out my second session of ADDLs, having completed six on 30 June using the mobile mirror that was set up on RAF Honiley's duty runway. I was the second detail, and the Squadron pilots were by the runway commenting on the success of the ADDLs that had been conducted by those on the first detail. I remember that nearly all were reckoned to be 5–10 knots faster than

110

Opposite page: WP302 in 1833 Squadron markings while with the Aircraft Holding Unit at RNAS Abbotsinch. The sets of louvres around the tailpipe, characteristic only of later-service Attackers, appear here to have been sealed off against the weather. Another late external modification, cooling intakes along the fuselage just forward of the tail fillet, is clearly in evidence.
Above: Sub-Lieutenant David Edwards approaches his aircraft during the Squadron's Annual Training at Ford in 1956. The red nose flashes first introduced by 800 Squadron were enthusiastically adopted by 1833; some incorporated the Squadron crest (as shown in the previous photograph).
Below: 1833 Squadron aircraft undergoing maintenance at Honiley. The aircraft in the foreground has its nose cap removed, revealing the G.45 gun camera installation; that in the background is WZ299. Most (though not all) of the Squadron's Attackers had their belly tanks identified by means of a single bold numeral, as can be seen here.

the required 100–105 knots, and I was determined to get the speed exactly right. The Attacker was not an easy aircraft to fly slowly: it did not 'talk' to us as did our beloved Sea Furies, in which, at 92 knots, a very slight tremor could be felt through the stick and a small amount of extra throttle did the trick.

The Attacker had a laminar-flow wing and the Pilot's Notes stated that there was 'slight airframe buffeting some 10 knots above [the stall]' and 'approximately 3–4 knots above the stall there is also slight aileron snatching.' I was unaware of this warning during the flight in question. My Attacker, WP283, had been refuelled after the first detail

Above: Six Attackers of 1832 Squadron in formation
Opposite, top: WP275 of the Southern Air Division (1832 Squadron). This RNVR unit was based at RAF Benson as an FAA 'lodger' squadron.
Right: A pair of SAD Attackers undergo inspection on the flight line at Benson. Unlike the two other RNVR Attacker units, this Division appears not to have 'decorated' the noses of its aircraft.

and had a full drop tank, which was standard practice; I cannot remember ever flying an Attacker 'clean'. I had experienced some problems picking up the lights and keeping the aircraft exactly on the approach path during my first session two weeks earlier, and this second session was proving to present the same sorts of difficulties.

My first approach was not comfortable. I remember trying to line up the lights and delaying paying attention to the ASI until very late on the approach. I applied full power to abort but it seemed to me at the time that the air sucked into the engine intakes was killing some of the lift on the inboard sections of the wings. The aircraft stalled short of the runway and finished up on the runway centre line in a seriously damaged condition. It never flew again. Amazingly, nothing caught fire, even though the drop tank took most of the impact because the undercarriage had departed as the aircraft hit the ground.

The runway in use was 24, and immediately before the threshold was a public road on which two young boys were watching our efforts. One of them was unfortunately killed as I crashed, and so the accident immediately became a disaster. I shall always be grateful to the Coroner at the Civil Inquest and to Commander Godfrey Place VC, who was then on the Staff of the Admiral Commanding Reserves and who helped me through both the Inquest and the RN Board of Enquiry.

My fellow pilots were tremendously supportive. I was given a check-up by the Squadron doctor and was happy to be detailed to fly again the same afternoon. Later on it was decided that all pilots would stall their Attackers with a full drop tank to establish the exact speed before attempting ADDLS.

We never did receive Sea Hawks. Thanks to the Duncan Sandys edict that no more manned fighter aircraft would be needed, both the RNVR Air Branch and the Royal Auxiliary Air Force were disbanded in early 1957. My service flying ceased in December 1956 with a 1 hour 15 minute flight in WK336. I had completed 130 Attacker hours all told, and these had included a memorable sortie night flying from RNAS Ford when I had climbed to look down on London from 35,000 feet. It was a real privilege to have been a very small part of a very great Service.

MISCELLANEOUS UNITS

Right: An Attacker is given a fresh coat of paint at the premises of Airwork Services. Modern military paint shops are rather different in character! As a matter of completely incidental interest, the lower surfaces of the aircraft have been masked using surplus copies of *Reveille* (a publication that will mean something to those of a certain age) and the *Daily Express*. Along with the Fleet Requirements Unit at Hurn, the civilian-run Airwork company, based at RNAS Brawdy and St David's, took on a number of Attackers after they had been withdrawn from front-line service, employing them in a variety of FAA support rôles.

Above: The wreck of an Attacker long since departed from service, photographed at Brawdy in the early 1960s.
Right: The Attacker preserved at the Fleet Air Arm Museum at RNAS Yeovilton, with the crest of 803 Squadron and the name of the late (and much-respected) Lieutenant-Commander Colin Casperd forward of the intake.

114

ATTACKERS FOR EXPORT

Left: The only overseas customer for the Attacker was the Pakistani Air Force (or Royal Pakistani Air Force as it was known at the time), which received a batch of three dozen Mk 1s with the wing-fold mechanism and arrester hooks deleted. The aircraft were originally completed, and test-flown, with civil registrations, as shown here.

Above: A publicity photograph showing Pakistani Attackers at South Marston. In the distance, an early Royal Navy Attacker with a dark-coloured fin sits on Supermarine's compass-swinging base. The photograph across pages 66–67 of this book makes for an interesting comparison.
Right: A Pakistani Attacker with an RAF Gloster Meteor Mk 8 nearby.

Above: A further pre-delivery photograph of an RPAF Attacker. The aircraft remained in their natural metal finish; the national markings were green and white. All the aircraft had the later-style, heavily framed cockpit hood.
Below: Two photographs of Attackers in PAF service, the nearest aircraft revealing some details of its Nene engine. The aircraft were assigned to No 11 Squadron, based at Mauripur (now called Masroor) near Karachi, and entered service on 1 June 1951—that is, almost three months before the first front-line FAA squadron was formed on the type. They were withdrawn from operations in 1956, replaced by North American F-86 Sabres. In the photograph immediately below, a Bristol Type 170 Freighter can also be seen.